The ETHICS of DELIBERATE DEATH

Kennikat Press
National University Publications
Multi-disciplinary Studies in the Law

Advisory Editor
Honorable Rudolph J. Gerber

The

ETHICS

of

DELIBERATE DEATH

EIKE-HENNER W. KLUGE

National University Publications
KENNIKAT PRESS // 1981
Port Washington, N.Y. // London

Copyright © 1981 by Kennikat Press Corp. All rights reserved. No
part of this publication may be reproduced, stored in a retrieval
system, or transmitted, in any form or by any means, electronic,
mechanical, photocopying, recording, or otherwise, without the
prior written permission of the publisher.

Manufactured in the United States of America

Published by
Kennikat Press Corp.
Port Washington, N.Y. / London

Library of Congress Cataloging in Publication Data

Kluge, Eike-Henner W
    The ethics of deliberate death.

    (Multi-disciplinary studies in law) (National
university publications)
    Bibliography: p.
    Includes index.
    1. Euthanasia. I. Title.
R726.K58   174'.24   80-36834
ISBN 0-8046-9260-2

CONTENTS

For my parents

The ETHICS of DELIBERATE DEATH

ABOUT THE AUTHOR

Eike-Henner W. Kluge is Associate Professor of Philosophy at the University of Victoria in British Columbia. He is the author of *The Practice of Death* (1975), various articles on medical ethics in journals and anthologies, and numerous publications in the history of philosophy of mathematics and logic.

INTRODUCTION

Our society is caught in a cultural revolution which is no less profound for being bloodless. The upheaval is all around us. In sexual mores the old attitudes have largely been replaced by the new, and the repercussions of this change are beginning to manifest themselves. In male-female roles and orientation the transition is still in full swing, but the new patterns will affect both the individual and the family. The emergence of the single parent as an accepted institution is here only one example. In areas such as the nature of criminality and the conception of the state the changes have barely begun, but if the increasing rejection of justice as retribution and the phenomenon of the urban guerilla are anything to go by they will be staggering in their ramifications.

The ultimate outcome of this revolution is unclear but its direction is not: We have entered upon a period of social fragmentation. No longer is a person defined in terms of the functions and roles he fulfils in society; rather his individuality and uniqueness as a person are fundamental, and his roles are acquired and extraneous, non-defining adjuncts to be discarded at will.

It is tempting to seek the reason for this in our changed economic conditions, our material wealth. This does identify important changes, but the real reason lies much deeper. We are faced with a fundamental identity crisis. We are reviewing the very notion of personhood: What is it to be a person? And what—if anything—follows from it? These questions lie at the heart of the current crisis, which because our culture is based on the notion of personhood, has thrown our whole system into turmoil.

Of course, crises of such proportions do not occur overnight or without reason. Why should it have occurred at this particular time in our history? For that matter, why should it have occured at all?

The answer is complicated, but the following can be identified as contributing parameters: a scientific revolution that began over two generations ago, a concurrent shift in our culture's basic philosophy, and a burgeoning sophistication in medical knowledge and techniques.

The scientific revolution has brought about a shift in some of our basic premises, much as it did historically in the Renaissance. At that time man lost his theologically guaranteed position as the focus of divine creation and became merely another biological unit in an infinite material world. Although little more gifted—perhaps even uniquely so—and a little better equipped than others to survive as a species, he was no longer a focal spark of divine fire but had lost his cosmic significance.

We, too, have altered our basic world view. Relativistic physics has replaced Newtonian mechanics; quantum theory has replaced the classical conception of the universe as causally predictable and has injected an ineluctable element of uncertainty into the heart of reality itself. We no longer have absolutes; only frames of reference. Partly in response to this, wholly new disciplines have arisen, such as sociology, anthropology, and economics. With few exceptions, all have their focus in man—*But not in man as an individual*. The phenomenon of individual indeterminacy already familiar from the physical sciences has also shown itself to hold true in the human context. While the individual person—the atomic constituent of humanity, so to speak—has proved largely inaccessible to scientific consideration and study, he has proved amenable to statistical analysis which expresses and even predicts his behaviour. He therefore no longer needs to be considered even as an individual. He has been reduced to part of a general mass of data to be dealt with in statistical terms.

These factors—loss of confidence in a predictable universe and loss of individuality—by themselves could have fomented a radical upheaval in our society and provoked a fundamental reappraisal of the significance of personhood *tout court*. However, they have been augmented by two other developments: the tremendous increase in our medical expertise and knowledge and a basic change in our philosophical orientation. The two are related: Medicine has successfully detailed, explained, and regulated our bodily functions; at the same time a whole pharmacopoeia of psyche-altering drugs and surgical techniques have spectacularly demonstrated medical control over our mental processes and has thrown into glaring relief the fact that the mental and the material sides of man are not separate spheres. Thus the success of the physical sciences has brought to a head the problem of man's essential nature.

Historically the nature of man has had two rival explanations, the one materialistic, the other dualistic. Both agreed that to be a person is, minimally, to be capable of self-awareness. They disagreed, however, in how this was to be spelled out. According to the materialistic tradition, awareness was simply a state of the physical body, perhaps of certain organs. If that ceased to be, then no person existed either. The dualistic tradition agreed that self-awareness was the crucial element in personhood; however, it maintained that self-awareness comes from the soul or spirit, rather than the physical body. Because it is difficult to tell when this soul is present and thus when an individual is a person, the dualistic tradition has generally followed the materialistic one in accepting whatever medical or other criteria the latter has proposed—with the understanding, of course, that these are merely criteria for the presence or absence of a soul, not criteria definitive of personhood itself.

For most of our cultural history the dualistic approach, associated as it was in the popular mind with the established religions, was dominant. However, relating medical knowledge to this decidedly incorporeal concept of personhood made for a very uneasy situation. Since a fundamental change in each could affect the other, any basic new development in either would have tremendous consequences.

One of these has in fact occurred. The developments in neurology and physiology have shown unequivocally that awareness, or consciousness, is a function of the central nervous system, specifically of the neocortex of the brain. This has prompted a return to materialistic theories and a refurbishing of what in the past had been somewhat naive mind-body identity theories. In short, materialism has become dominant over the dualism of old.

With this, of course, the notion of what it is to be a person has also undergone a fundamental reorientation, and the process of exploring the sociocultural, legal, and ethical implications of this change has begun. It is the repercussions of this that are just beginning to be felt.

Especially implicated is the finite nature of human life. While the dualistic tradition was dominant, death occasioned little worry. It was seen merely as the transition from an embodied to a disembodied state, and any social significance it had dealt with the life hereafter. For the materialistic tradition, however, matters stand otherwise. For it death is the final end, "the horror of the shade." Therefore the transition to a materialistic outlook prompted new attitudes towards life. A here-and-now attitude began to acquire dominance. The individual person came to see himself as evanescent and fragile. A natural outcome of this in turn— natural in the sense of "to be expected"—was the desire to ensure and defend both his existence and individuality for as long as possible. He instinctively desired the continuation of that frail self.

The results of these changes were not long in coming. Laws predicated on the old dualistic conception of personhood—laws which saw death as having a teaching function even for the individual himself—began to be scrutinized. A fascination with death arose. To be sure, we have not become thanatophiles, enamoured of death and dying, but death in its various guises has assumed a prominent place in our thought. The intensity and ubiquity of the debate over the death of a fetus in abortion, the aged in senicide, and the critically ill and hopelessly and agonizingly deformed in infanticide and euthanasia all bear witness to this.

Nor was the effect of the ascendence of the materialistic notion of personhood confined to the appraisal of death. Since the body itself has become the person, the woman who claims a moral and legal right to an abortion because it concerns her body emerges as claiming nothing other than a right to her own identity: to the integrity of her person. At the same time she is not deterred by competing claims made on behalf of the fetus because by those very materialistic criteria of personhood it is *not yet* a person and therefore has no competing rights.

With this arises another fundamental development: the notion of personhood *as a problem*. The distinction between a person and a human being, which previously was unimportant or even absent, now becomes significant. Mere membership in the species homo sapiens or mere possession of a living human body no longer guarantees personhood. The functions of that body such as self-awareness, language, and volition, particularly in their neurophysiological ramifications, now play a defining role.

For the individual caught in these countercurrents there are practical complications. While we live in an age of medical miracles and relative material abundance (at least in our own society) and while medical sophistication can hold off death for quite some time, these resources are not universally available even here: There is still a relative scarcity of medical resources.

This raises the question of right: Who has a right to lifesaving or sustaining medical care—even to any medical care? Under what circumstances and conditions does he have that right? The problems assume particularly poignant and depressing dimensions when we note that certain terminal, comatose, and irreparably brain-damaged individuals in the intensive care wards of our hospitals are in fact no longer persons according to the new criteria even though their bodies are still alive. The question therefore arises whether care for these individuals should be continued or whether we should practise euthanasia in one form or another—actively by direct intervention, or passively and indirectly by "letting nature take its course"—so that those who are still persons might benefit from the resources thus liberated and have a chance to live. In other words, the sociolegal issue of rights has become tied to the philosophical issue of personhood and to the question of medical ethics.

The situation is complicated still further by the deep-rooted human desire to avoid pain and suffering expressed in the wish for a "fair and easy passage" should death be inevitable. When modern medicine prolongs life it may well be in accord with the universal desire for continued self-existence, but it may also prolong the indignity and suffering that people abhor. Medical techniques and services, where they have been available, have traditionally been applied almost automatically in order to sustain life, sometimes even against the wishes of the patient. However, the growing realization that death is ultimately personal, the extinction of the self, and that modern medicine can keep the individual alive long beyond the threshold of pain or the hope of meaningful recovery calls forth an instinctive reaction based on the desire to avoid meaningless pain. This manifests itself in a vociferous insistence on the right to death. The claim is made that the right to death is logically entailed by the constitutionally guaranteed right to life. It is then argued that anyone who is caught in a state of protracted terminal suffering, who is agonized, helpless, or drugged almost to the point of stupor and whose hope of recovery is nil, should be allowed to exercise his right to death; and that those who are in a similar position but are unable to claim this right—perhaps due to coma or because they are no longer compos mentis—should be allowed to die if there is any previous indication that they would have wished it.

Obviously this emphasis on the supremacy of the individual's control over his life is fostered by and feeds on the increasingly granular, individual-oriented structure of society. It is equally as obvious that this self-orientation lets considerations of the greatest good for the greatest number of people fade in importance before the individual good.

Legislation recognizing the right to voluntary euthanasia is now on the agenda of several legislatures. Whatever the practical implications of this may be for the moment—the California Natural Death Act shows that at least the initial attempts at legislation will be neither entirely clear nor entirely successful—the direction in which we are moving seems apparent.

While this sort of move is to be welcomed as an attempt to provide clarity on a crucially important issue, it is also to be feared; it is fraught with danger. The very factors that make a review of legislation necessary if the new moral sentiments are to find statutory expression are still too little appreciated and the situation itself is still too fluid to allow for cogent, coherent, and above all morally acceptable legislation. Statutes have something like a life of their own. Once enacted and proclaimed, they are very difficult to change. The danger therefore is that legislation of this sort, although in many ways necessary, will be too precipitate; that the legislation that has already been or is being drafted is but a reaction to the vociferous demands of various interest groups, with little attention being paid to the full philosophical import of what is at stake; and that what results may turn out to be a legislative monster that we are then powerless to change.

The problem of euthanasia is not a medical problem. It is not a matter of technical, medical decision-making about when or whether to use a certain drug or technique. Nor is it a socioeconomic problem—a question of the economics of a life-and-death situation, the finances of a protracted debility or terminal illness, the social impact of continued extensive care, or even the spectacle of undignified suffering. Nor, finally, does the issue focus on the legalities at stake. Unquestionably these are relevant and important issues. However, before all else the problem of euthanasia is a philosophical problem: the problem of the ethics of deliberate death. As such it incorporates several key philosophical issues: whether and to what degree a person has the right to the disposition of his life; the moral nature of the interrelationship between persons; their rights vis-à-vis those of society at large. Even more basically it involves the question of personhood *tout court*. For only when euthanasia deals with persons rather than mere biological organisms do we even have a problem. Only after it has been determined that it is morally justifiable to recall a patient in shock to an excruciatingly agonized existence as a cancer patient and to keep him alive as long as possible—if necessary, even against his own will—does it make sense to consider how to implement this decision medically or to support it legally. Only after it has been found morally acceptable to keep an irreparably and severely brain-damaged individual alive at all costs or to terminate an infant with Down's syndrome and duodenal atresia is it relevant to address the medical and legal whys and hows. Only after examination and resolution of the ethics of triage situations can we decide meaningfully who is to live and who is to die.

As time goes on, the problem of the individual's right or duty to die will assume greater and greater importance, especially if the current socioeconomic trends continue and the availability of medical resources decreases rather than increases. Laws governing the distribution of these resources will become not merely desirable but necessary. Whereas the unexamined life may not be worth living, the unexamined law will make it either unbearable or impossible. A full awareness of the various moral issues involved is therefore a sine qua non of rational procedure. It is my hope that the pages that follow will contribute towards achieving that end.

1

THE ACT OF EUTHANASIA

Complex, often confusing, and usually emotional, contemporary discussions of euthanasia assail us with a variety of approaches and conclusions. Some arguments oppose it, others condone it, and still others advocate it outright. Some stigmatize it as murder, others characterize it as a kind of suicide, and still others present it simply as an extension of the right to death. It has been described as a medical, moral, and even religious issue, and arguments variously focus on socioeconomic, political, historical, cultural, and psychological factors. The dispassionate observer must sometimes feel that there are as many different approaches as there are individual participants in the debate.

This diversity of opinion derives its urgency and emotional thrust from a practical concern. All of us sooner or later face extinction. The complication is that most deaths in our society occur in a hospital setting and under circumstances that present a real option: to continue to live for some time through the agency of mechanical devices, drugs, and resuscitative and sustaining techniques or to die without any effort being expended beyond making as "fair and easy" a passage as possible under the circumstances. Most of us will be confronted with this option. In some cases the issue will even reduce to the question of whether, as the poet Rilke put it in *The Book of Poverty and Death*, we have a right to "our own death." For many of us, therefore, the problem of euthanasia is really a personal question: How will our lives end? Above all, however, it is a moral issue. Clarifying the problem is therefore necessary as well as worthwhile.

Arguments about euthanasia differ in four general areas. There are differences in basic moral premises, in factual premises, in reasoning, and in the interpretation of the various terms. A difference in basic moral premises is of course fundamental, but it is also difficult to identify. Not that it is hard to point out the basic moral tenets professed by those who advance the various arguments or to identify the ethical premises on which their conclusions are supposedly based. These tenets are frequently, vociferously, and publicly enunciated, and the ethical premises are not less openly put forth. Rather the difficulty is that the tenets that are publicly professed are not always those that are employed in the construction of the arguments, and the alleged ethical premises are not always ethical in nature—or for that matter, the real basis of the reasoning. Of course they may be as they appear, but the problem of euthanasia is too important to be settled on the basis of assumptions. We must look and see. Only when the basic moral premises have been identified can we evaluate their acceptability. Similarly, only when the various strands of the arguments have been disentangled can we be sure of their factual premises and determine their correctness. Furthermore, the complexity of these strands may hide very deep logical and conceptual confusions. This is all the more likely since euthanasia is an emotionally charged topic that may easily present as rational reasons what are really emotional associations and lend an air of logical cogency to what in fact is only emotionally persuasive.

An investigation into the arguments would therefore pinpoint the actual moral and factual premises that underlie the reasoning. If these differences turn out to be factual they may then at least in principle be resolved. On the other hand, if they turn out to be moral we will be confronted with the bare fact of our moral disagreement. The opposition over which premises are right and which are wrong may then remain firmly entrenched, but the reverse may also happen: What seemed to be a solid moral premise in the context of a particular argument may turn out to be exceedingly dubious when considered in and by itself; and what appeared to be wholly acceptable in its argumentative context may upon cool and reasoned examination, separated from what we should like to prove, strike us as wholly unacceptable. Thus, simply clarifying the differences in reasoning may also have a persuasive effect. However, all this depends on a clear understanding of the terms used and on precision in their interpretation.

EUTHANASIA

Participants in the discussion over the morality of euthanasia do not always understand the same thing by the term "euthanasia." It is used in various ways and contexts whose differences may be morally relevant and significant. Can we identify a common meaning for "euthanasia"?

The expectation that we can easily do so, fostered by definition of it in the *Shorter Oxford English Dictionary* as "a quiet and easy death" or the action of producing "a quiet and easy death," is soon dashed by a look at the several apparently contradictory meanings in common usage: *Positive euthanasia* supposedly amounts to bringing about the easy death of an individual directly but not by omission; Robert Veatch defines *negative euthanasia* as "letting [the individual] die by withholding treatment" and calls *indirect euthanasia* bringing about the death of the individual not as the primary and intended result of a particular (usually pain-relieving) action but as an accompanying and secondary effect; J. R. Connery distinguishes between *passive euthanasia*, which is to be considered not as "an act of killing, . . . as death suffered by incurable disease, without suffering; [i.e., it is] allowing the patient to die in comfort"; and *active euthanasia*, which by contrast he characterizes as the "taking [of] active measures to end [the patient's] life." *Voluntary euthanasia* is sometimes understood as euthanatizing at the request of the patient here and now or on the basis of an expressed wish that is still in force, and *euthanasia* itself is taken to mean all acts of euthanasia that are not thus voluntary in nature. Euthanasia has even been construed by Connery to mean "the failure to supply ordinary means" to save or sustain someone's life. And these are but a few of a myriad of different uses.

Nevertheless, these various uses are not necessarily contradictory since in all except the last the different meanings involved are a result of the qualifying adjectives that accompany the term. Presumably, therefore, once these are removed there will remain a conceptual core: Euthanasia can basically be defined as the act of bringing about the death of a person in order to prevent his suffering. The morality of this "bringing about" is of course another matter. However, emotional associations and moral preconceptions so encrust the term as to be mistaken for the term itself. Therefore in this book the term appears in the sense familiar from legal contexts as enunciated in *Black's Law Dictionary*, Revised Fourth Edition: "the art or practice of painlessly putting to death persons suffering from incurable and distressing disease." Having this systematic meaning allows us to investigate the nature of euthanasia without inherent moral bias.

ACTIVE EUTHANASIA AND PASSIVE EUTHANASIA

A common-assertion in discussions of euthanasia is that actively doing something in order to bring about the demise of an individual is different from letting him die by withdrawing relevant medical services or not using them in the first place. The claim is that the former is morally reprehensible but that the latter is not. As Sade and Redfern put it for the medical profession,

. . . Passive euthanasia is not an act of killing, it is death suffered by incurable disease, without suffering. . . . Active termination of life . . . is an act of killing, and no humanitarian rationalization can make it morally defensible. . . . There is profound moral difference between allowing a patient to die of his disease in comfort [passive euthanasia] and taking active measures to end his life [active euthanasia].

The prominent protestant theologian Paul Ramsey argues:

In omissions no human agent causes the patient's death, directly or indirectly. He dies his own death from causes that it is no longer merciful or reasonable to fight. . . . In any case, doing something and omitting something in order to do something else are different sorts of acts. To do or not to do something may, then, be different sorts of acts. One may be wrong and the other may be right, even if these decisions and actions are followed by the same end result, namely the death of a patient.

The difference between the two modes of action, therefore, seems well entrenched and clear. But is it? And is it cogent?

The passages just quoted contend that failures to act are not themselves acts and that, moreover, they have an entirely different moral status. However, both theses are mistaken. The thesis that a failure to act is not itself an act equates an act with what in the end amounts to an expenditure of energy and maintains that as long as an individual does not expend any energy to alter the causal flow of events, he has not acted.

However, this equation is mistaken—at least in its generality—and so are the inferences based on it. Not only everyday life but also the law recognizes this fact in the concept of culpable negligence. As Otto Kirchheimer points out, "A man who caused another to be drowned by refusing to hold out his hand would in common language be said to have killed him"; and although the "drowning is neither brought about nor accelerated by the passive attitude of the bystander" it could have been prevented by the action that is morally expected. Therefore, there is "no difference between the causality of omission and of positive action, and the same rules, or absence of rules, which govern commission apply to omission." The point is that an act is what determines the causal flow of events—how things happen—and that this does not necessitate physical activity or expenditure of energy. For the flow of events may be determined either by an expenditure of energy so as to ensure that the events follow each other in a certain sequence or by the failure to exert any energy. Whether or not something is a cause therefore, is really the question of whether or not it is instrumental in determining the possibilities inherent in a particular situation in a specific way. This point may also be put by saying that the causal structure of any situation involves a set of possibilities and that this set of possibilities is determined to a single one by the causal determination of the individual who finds himself at the decision point. That determination may involve the active removal or blocking of all possibilities save one; or it may consist of non-interference with the already established play of causal forces so as to allow a specific possibility to be realized precisely in virtue of his non-interference.

The thesis that failures to act are not acts is therefore mistaken. The failure to act is nevertheless an act because it too is the determination of a given sequence of events. In failing to hold out my hand to the drowning person, in failing to rush a diver with explosive decompression to a decompression chamber I make just as sure that a certain established sequence of causal events will continue as when I fail to remove the duodenal atresia of the infant with Down's syndrome, refuse a heart-lung machine to the critically stricken patient or life-sustaining medication to the incurably, chronically, and agonizingly ill. In these and similar cases the failure to act constitutes the determination of the line of development of events. If that failure is intentional, then it constitutes a deliberate act, its non-physical nature notwithstanding. The notion of an act includes both physical action and non-action. Therefore, if an act has moral dimensions then an individual cannot escape these simply by pointing out that he did not expend any energy, for moral praise and blame do not attach to an expenditure of energy as such but to the determination of a causal situation. On the other hand, they do not attach to any and all such determinations but only to those which Aristotle in his *Nicomachean Ethics* characterized as voluntary or deliberate. Thus, deliberately withholding action while being aware that action is possible constitutes a conscious attempt to determine what happens. Such an inaction therefore has the same moral status as an overt physical activity. Both common sense and the law recognize this fact and, as Kirchheimer puts it, place "omissions on the same footing as wilful acts." Whence it follows that the active-passive distinction is of no moral significance here and that what is called passive euthanasia is just as much in the domain of morally judgable acts as what is called active euthanasia. It is not enough to say with Veatch that the failure to use supportive or saving measures "is in no sense a positive cause of death." The real question is, is this failure a deliberate determinant of death *at all*? And if the answer is yes, then it must be evaluated on a moral basis like any other such act. Certainly to reason like Ramsey that "in omission no agent causes the patient's death" is simply to be mistaken, if the statement is construed as a general principle.

INDIRECT EUTHANASIA

Direct and indirect euthanasia in ordinary usage are frequently taken to be synonymous with active and passive euthanasia, but they are actually quite distinct. As we saw, both active euthanasia and passive euthanasia are acts, and being deliberate determinations of the course of events are subject to moral evaluation. Direct and indirect euthanasia are also deliberate determinations of what happens. However, what characterizes indirect euthanasia as opposed to passive euthanasia is not the way in which the course of events is determined but the *causal distance* between the act and the final outcome and the number of *contributory conditions* necessary to bring it about. An example would be administering a specific drug that results in certain chemical imbalances in the body of a patient which finally lead to his death. The former leads to the latter—determines it, as it were—despite the causal distance intervening. Similarly, a number of contributory conditions are involved when an analgesic narcotic is administered repeatedly in doses sufficiently large to relieve pain but having as an unfortunate side effect the death of the patient. Although each administration by itself does not cause the death of the patient, together they determine his demise. The distinction between direct and indirect euthanasia, therefore, does not coincide with the active-passive distinction since indirect euthanasia may result from either action or failure to act.

This, of course, still leaves the moral question: Is the indirect act subject to moral evaluation? It may not be, but only under certain conditions and not invariably. Thus, with respect to indirectness in distance, what is normally foreseeable plays a very important role. If what intervenes is foreseeable and likely to occur in the normal course of events, then the moral gravamen of the initial act will not be lessened by its distance from the final result. To take a particular example: It is normally foreseeable that when the electricity for an oxygenator is turned off the latter will stop functioning. It is also normally foreseeable that if a patient who depended for his survival on the proper functioning of the oxygenator were suddenly to be deprived of its efficient operation or if that operation were halted altogether the patient would die. The action of throwing the switch, therefore, although not a direct cause of the patient's death, nevertheless would have his death as its normally foreseeable result. Consequently the moral gravamen attaching to that act would not be lessened by its distance from the final result even if that result should be some time in the making.

Correspondingly, euthanasia that is indirect in that it invites a number of contributory conditions does not necessarily lose its moral substance.

Thus a particular dose of a certain medicament may bring about death only if certain other conditions are simultaneously present—say, a particular degree or type of debilitation or the presence of certain other drugs in the body at the time. However, if whoever administers the medicament knows or suspects that this condition is present or could normally expect it to be so, then the moral dimensions of administering the medicament are not affected by the causal complexity of the situation.

Therefore neither distance nor the number of conditions involved necessarily affect the moral weight of an action. It might be condemned or regarded with moral approbation, but not on these grounds. Nor does ignorance of what is normally to be expected in a given context constitute an escape clause. As Aristotle pointed out in his *Nicomachean Ethics,*

Even ignorance is in itself no protection against punishment if a person is thought to be responsible for his ignorance . . . . punishment is inflicted for offences committed in ignorance of such provisions of the law [and of facts] as the offender ought to have known or might easily have known. It is also inflicted in other cases in which ignorance seems to be due to negligence: *it was in the offender's power not to be ignorant*, it is argued, *and he could have made sure had he wanted to.*

A physician or nurse *ought* to be aware of the patient's condition before administering or withdrawing certain drugs or services; *ought* to be aware of what normally ensues upon the administration of a certain medicament or failure to administer it. Ignorance of these is negligence in the execution of duty; and such negligence can scarcely be a reason for changing one's moral judgment to the positive. Furthermore, these considerations apply not only to what one could normally expect to happen in the usual course of events but also to what the people involved in these situations might or could normally be expected to *do*.

To sum up, if an act of euthanasia is morally unacceptable as it stands, it cannot be made morally acceptable by showing it to be indirect; and if an act of indirect euthanasia is morally acceptable its acceptability does not reside in its indirectness.

Wherein does its moral acceptability reside? Either in the nature of the act, the circumstances that surround it, or some moral principle.

THE PRINCIPLE OF DOUBLE EFFECT

One of the concepts frequently used to justify what would otherwise be considered a morally objectionable act of euthanasia is the principle of double effect. This principle is best known from the context of abortion situations where saving the life of the mother must entail killing the fetus. There it supposedly shows that this killing, which would otherwise be morally objectionable, does not contravene moral and theological tenets. Callahan holds that "the indicated medical procedure to save the life of the mother . . . has as its direct intention the saving of the life of the mother; the death of the fetus is the foreseen but unintended and indirect result of the life saving surgery performed on the mother." In situations involving euthanasia the principle finds expression in arguments like the following, to be found in *Ethical and Religious Directives for Catholic Health Facilities*, no. 28: "It is not euthanasia to give a dying person sedatives and analgesics for the alleviation of pain, when such a measure is judged necessary, even though they may shorten [the patient's] life." Other sources suggest that applying this principle may even result in a morally acceptable death. Thus *On Dying Well* argues that "Destruction will be morally justifiable only if the good sought outweighs the evil done and only if that good cannot be secured in any other less destructive way."

The principle itself is that if one act has two consequences, the one good and the other evil, where both consequences are inevitable outcomes of the initial act itself, then the act is morally acceptable (and, presumably, the bad result morally excusable) if these four conditions are met:

(1) Considered in and by itself, the act as such is not morally objectionable.

(2) The agent's intention in performing the act is directed towards the good to be achieved only and does not include the bad result as a desideratum.

(3) The bad result is merely the inevitable concomitant and not a means to the good result or a condition of it.

(4) There are grave reasons for engaging in the act itself such that failure to perform the act would result in at least as bad a state of affairs as the bad effect of the performance of the act.

The application of the principle to justify euthanasia is relatively clear. The cases fall into two general categories: those involving an element of triage and those focusing on the agonizing, "undignified" but in any case irremediable condition of the patient. In the case of triage the reasoning is this: Since by the very nature of the situation it is impossible to save both individuals by supplying adequate medical care; and since the non-distribution as well as equal distribution of the available resources will result in the death of both, the selective allocation of the resources (and the pleasant or at least painless demise of one of the individuals) is justified by all four conditions. In situations involving irremediable agony, that state is used as the grave reason for justifying the administration of an analgesic (or other appropriate drug or technique) in amounts that will appreciably shorten the life of the individual or even kill him outright then and there.

If correct, the principle would determine the morality not only of this sort of euthanasia but also of all situations involving double-resultant acts where one effect is good and another evil, even in those situations that do not involve a lethal denouement. It could, for instance, be used to justify keeping a person alive even though that entailed as an undesirable side effect his unbearable agony or degrading existence.

However, the principle is ultimately unacceptable because it is inherently incoherent. The morally acceptable act itself presents no difficulty. But the condition that the agent's intention in performing the act must not include as a desideratum the accompanying bad result cannot be met consistently with the other conditions.

Why is this so? It is already clear that an act in itself is not identical with the physical activity that may be involved in performing it. Thus, the act of murdering a person is not identical with the physical activity of slipping a knife into his heart, the act of stealing is not identical with that of taking certain goods, and so on. In all these cases the mere physical activity must be the result of intention and must occur in a certain context. In fact, all other things being equal, the nature and identity of a given act resides precisely in its context and in the person's intention. Someone may stumble, have a muscle spasm, or simply be careless; he may take something by accident or be a kleptomaniac. Without these conditions—or with different ones operative—the acts would be different.

Since this holds for acts in general, the act referred to in the second clause above is no exception. Being an act, it too takes its nature and identity from the context and the intention associated with it. That fact, however, calls into question the very first requirement, the moral acceptability of the act. For the same act must meet all four conditions. But the moral status of the act referred to in the second clause is precisely the double-resultant act whose moral status is here in question. Therefore, in characterizing it as morally acceptable, the first condition begs the question at issue since it is in the nature of the act that it be double-resultant and involve the particular intention of bringing about the good result despite the bad.

This introduces the second difficulty: The intention can never be confined solely to effecting the good result without the bad. This is so because the agent must be at least aware of the results of the action in order to evaluate the requisite grave reasons. Otherwise, the whole clause would be meaningless and the argument collapse. Furthermore, in this situation the bad result is inevitable. (Otherwise the problem would be entirely different.) Therefore given the agent's awareness of this close connection between good and bad results, his intention in performing the act cannot be confined to bringing about the good result only but must include the bad as well.

This, however, does not mean that the bad result must therefore be the agent's primary objective. It merely entails that it must be part of his intention, something that he would rather not see happen but that he prefers to bring about instead of some other still less acceptable state of affairs. But for that very reason it is impossible for the agent not to intend the bad result at all. The *only* thing that is possible for double-resultant acts under the conditions specified is that the agent intend to bring about the good result in spite of the bad and in preference to some other even less acceptable state of affairs.

To sum up the dilemma: Either the morally acceptable act of the first condition is not the same act mentioned in the other clauses and the argument therefore becomes invalid; or this act is indeed the morally pregnant act of the other clauses, in which case to call it morally acceptable begs the question. Furthermore, the condition of limited intention cannot be met and hence the argument could never find application in practice. Neither alternative is acceptable. Therefore the principle fails.

Finally, it should be noted that the whole principle of double effect involves an inherent appeal to the general moral principle of utility, or the principle of greatest good for the greatest number. While this is not a logical reason for rejecting it, that principle is essentially confused and unacceptable, as will become clear later. Therefore, even if the preceding analysis were faulty the principle of double effect would still not establish anything about the moral status of an act of euthanasia.

ORDINARY MEANS AND EXTRAORDINARY MEANS

The distinction between ordinary means and extraordinary means used to preserve life rocketed to theological prominence when Pope Pius XII, speaking before the 1957 International Congress of Anaesthesiologists, took the stand that

. . . morally one is held to use only ordinary means—according to the circumstances of persons, places, times and cultures—that is to say, means that do not involve any grave burden for oneself or another. A more strict obligation would be too burdensome for most men and would render the attainment of the higher, more important good too difficult. . . . On the other hand, one is not forbidden to take more than the strictly necessary steps to preserve life and health, as long as he does not fail in some more serious duty.

Directive No. 28 of the *Ethical and Religious Directives for Catholic Health Facilities* restated the position and Connery took it one step further by holding that, "If there is no obligation to initiate extraordinary means, there is no obligation to continue them. One does not assume an obligation to continue to use such means by beginning to use them." The point at issue here is the notion supposedly explicated: the distinction between ordinary and extraordinary means itself. This supposedly specific and precise distinction is fairly ambiguous: What is considered extraordinary is inherently relative from context to context, time to time, and even culture to culture and also within a given culture even where contexts and resources are similar. There is the inescapable personal variable.

In recognition of this, various writers have attempted to make the distinction particular and specific. Preston Williams calls extraordinary means those that are "very costly, or very painful, or very difficult, or very dangerous"; others seize on the likelihood of success in saving the life of the patient or concentrate on what are considered to be the prevailing medical standards.

However the relativity and ambiguity that marked the original distinction remain. What is painful for one may be excruciating for another and only slightly bothersome to a third—but not all of the time and under the same circumstances and not even for the same person. What may be usual in one context need not be so in another; the various degrees of "usualness" may seem intuitively obvious in one case, but for all that they do not carry any guarantee of certainty with them and are impossible to quantify or fix in the manner necessary for repeated, consistent usage. Even the intuitions of practice do not seem to engender agreement. Thus, while some consider the use of oxygen extraordinary and unusual others mention only hemodialysis or continued intravenous feeding in this light. And what of pacemakers? Open heart surgery? Heart or kidney transplants? Cut-downs? The list could go on.

If these considerations are any indication, then the notion of unusualness and of extra-ordinariness in the end turns out to be a function of medical sophistication and expertise and of the willingness not to be inconvenienced too easily. But as Marya Mannes has put it so accurately, this makes the distinction itself "conveniently ambiguous." As to the concept of prevailing standards, it too is characterized by this dangerous imprecision: By whom are they defined? In what context? With what purpose and justification? Are they absolutely and consistently applicable without qualification? Who and what decides the exceptions? Difficulties could be multiplied. The criterion of the likelihood of saving a life may be thought to fare somewhat better, but here too problems arise. What sort of life? As a decerebrated neomort? An incurably stricken and agonized human wreck? A functioning cripple? Or as a normally healthy and above all sane person? The gradation is as extensive as it is continuous. Where is the line to be drawn?

Objections to the distinction between ordinary and extraordinary means are not confined to this quarter. More specifically, there are objections to its moral thrust. For the whole distinction rests on the general assumption that the norm (or what is taken to be the norm) in a particular domain of action is the rule of what ought to be done in that domain. The reasoning here focuses on what is somehow determined as being usual, ordinary, or standard procedure, identifies this as the norm of what is done, and then stamps it as the norm of what *ought* to be done. That constitutes a logical mistake. It is true that in some situations what is done is also what ought to be done and vice versa. However, this is so not of necessity but of happenstance. Furthermore, that the two happen to coincide is not a matter of statistical determination but because of the moral aspects of the case. What is done happens to agree with the moral precepts that are otherwise determined. Socrates knew the fallacy of arguing from what is to what ought to be done and of taking the former to be definitive of the latter; and he castigated the Sophists (who argued otherwise) for perverting the true order of things. Therefore while one particular practice may be considered "ordinary" and another not, this shows neither that the practices themselves are morally acceptable nor that they ought to be performed in the first place. Nor does it follow that if they are not "ordinary" in this particular context there is no obligation to employ them. Logically and morally the two are distinct.

Incidentally, if the reasoning underlying the distinction were to be accepted the impetus for developing new lifesaving technology would disappear. After all, if what is done—what is ordinary—is what ought to be done and nothing else is why should the situation be changed? That sort of reasoning, however, would stand in serious conflict with the generally accepted assumption that we have an obligation to try to help others by continuing to extend the boundaries of our techniques, drugs, and devices as far as possible.

Finally, the arguments from extraordinary means leave the uneasy feeling that a matter of convenience is being presented as a matter of moral fact. The distinction itself may be nothing but an attempt to come to grips with current practice in terms of what the medical community finds by and large convenient to do, and to accept this as the best that can and ought to be done. Convenience does not amount to duty, however, and practice is no guarantee of morality. Of course this feeling may be unjustified. Perhaps the whole point is that a human being can do only so much with any reasonable hope of success and that when this point has been passed there is no longer any obligation to continue.

However, if that is the point then it can be expressed more simply like this: There is no obligation to continue to try to achieve what is recognized to be unattainable under the circumstances; therefore in cases of hopelessly terminal illness there is no obligation to continue lifesaving or supportive measures. In that case, however, the real thrust of the distinction is not between what is ordinary and what is extraordinary but between what is likely to be successful and what is not: If the prognosis is for lack of success, then there is no obligation to engage in the action. This reasoning, however, is logically different and requires separate treatment.

NEGATIVE PROGNOSIS

A recent communication by the Bishops of the Federal Republic of Germany expresses quite clearly what in many medical situations of euthanasia seems to be an overriding criterion, the negative or positive prognosis:

As long as there is any possibility of the sick man recovering . . . it is obligatory to use all such measures (as respirator, etc.). Also, it is the duty of the state to ensure that even costly apparatus and expensive medicines are available for those who need them. It is quite another matter when all hope of recovery is ruled out and the use of particular medical techniques would only lengthen artificially what may be a painful death.

Paul Ramsey asserts that, "in judging whether to try any given treatment one has to estimate whether there is a reasonable hope of success in saving a man's life"; Pope Pius XII states that an anaesthesiologist is not morally bound to employ techniques of artificial respiration in situations that are deemed "completely hopeless"; and Gerald Kelly claims that we are morally obliged to employ ordinary means where these are defined as "all medicines, treatments, and operations, which offer a reasonable hope of benefit for the patient" and where "benefit for the patient" is defined as "what offers reasonable hope of success." The stance that is here adopted is clear, but the point is not always expressed quite so bluntly. Sometimes it is hidden by phrases like Kelly's "ordinary means" or Veatch's "reasonable practice" or even by purported considerations for the patient's dignity and his right to freedom from torture.

This camouflage apart, however, the thesis underlying these sentiments centres in the concept of a negative prognosis and may be expressed like this: An attempt to keep a patient alive is morally obligatory and indeed is rational if and only if there is a reasonable hope of success. To engage in lifesaving and/or sustaining endeavours when the prognosis is negative is not to act out of a duty—here there is none—but to act irrationally, solely out of a desire to assuage any feelings of guilt or failure that might otherwise exist. Because this would be a pointless waste of resources and an imposition on the patient, it would be better to refrain from initiating or continuing the medical intervention. Instead we should make the patient as comfortable as possible and let him die in peace. We incur no moral guilt by proceeding in this manner since the final outcome—death—is in any case a foregone conclusion.

The underlying principle here is simply a version of the general moral maxim that one cannot have a duty to do what it is impossible to do and that one cannot have a duty to try to do what is known to have an unsuccessful outcome from the very start. This principle is certainly acceptable, but its application here depends on ambiguous terms that may vitiate its usefulness. For instance, the notion of success is central to the principle's application, but how precisely is it to be understood? Keeping the patient alive? Medical technology can keep alive human bodies even with completely deteriorated brains (and in one case did so even when the brain had liquified). Effecting a complete cure from the particular debility or disease? That high a standard would make poliomyelitis victims euthanasia candidates and place "cured" patients with residual after-effects into the group of those who should be killed. Restoring the patient to the health of a more or less normally functioning member of society? But normalcy is relative, a function of what we as members of society are willing to accept. The mere absence of pain? That may be achieved in a variety of ways, none of which need have anything to do with "success." In short, what would here count as success is not at all clear, and different societies almost certainly operate with different yardsticks.

Furthermore, there are two different notions of success that must be clearly distinguished: successful outcome and successful action. A successful outcome means achieving a certain desired result, perhaps curing a disease or saving a life, that would not come about but for the performance of the act in question. The result is the reason for performing the act in the first place. However, in some situations achieving such a result, although unquestionably desirable, nevertheless is not what counts as success. Success here resides in the performance of the act itself. The difference between success considered as successful action and as successful outcome is enormous. It is illustrated in sports by the difference between the success of winning as opposed to the enjoyment and satisfaction inherent in playing the game. Bridge playing provides a similar distinction. But so does engaging in a profession. Here success may mean either the successful outcome of achieving a particular result (say, financial gain) or the successful action of fulfilling one's duty as a professional, e.g., as a lawyer to one's client. In situations where the outcome-oriented interpretation of "success" is inappropriate, success or lack thereof in the outcome-oriented sense is irrelevant with respect to the question of whether the individual from whom the act is demanded has an obligation to engage or continue to engage in it. For instance, a lawyer who refused to work for a bona fide client because of a negative prognosis of success would be derelict in his duty. This is because the client claims not the right to win—the right to a successful outcome—but the right to the professional's best efforts on his behalf. Therefore any claim that no such obligation on the part of the professional existed could not be established by pointing to the likelihood of losing (i.e., of failing). The lawyer would have to show that the client has no right to the professional's performance of the act in his behalf. This may be possible, but it certainly is not a foregone conclusion and involves quite different considerations. Of course, none of this invalidates the impossibility clause of the criterion of negative prognosis. It does mean, however, that if success refers to the action instead of the outcome, that the interpretation of "impossible" must be adjusted accordingly: It must then refer to the action and not the result. The principle would then read: If it is impossible to engage in the action in the necessary way, then there is no obligation to try to do so.

In euthanasia the criterion of negative prognosis (or impossibility of success) assumes that medical intervention is always outcome-oriented. From this it concludes that if the desired outcome is impossible (insofar as is humanly known) then there is no obligation to intervene. Saving the patient, not performing the act of medical intervention, is the standard of success in this interpretation. However, it cannot be assumed as a universal medical truism that medical intervention, or more precisely the obligation to engage in such, is always act-oriented so as to being about a "cure," to "arrest the progress of the disease," or to be efficacious in some such sense. Rather there is evidence that, by and large, the obligations of physician are like those of other professionals, e.g., like lawyers: act-oriented in nature. As D.A. Karnofsky recently put it,

It is ethically wrong for a doctor to make an arbitrary judgment, at a certain point in the patient's illness, to stop supportive measures. The patient entrusts his life to his doctor, and it is the doctor's duty to sustain it as long as possible. There should be no suggestion that it is possible for the doctor to do otherwise. . . .

As Hilda Regier also holds, "A patient is placed, or places himself, in the care of a physician with the expectation that he (the physician) will do *everything in his power, everything that is known to modern medicine*, to protect the patient's life." Here there is not even a hint of an outcome-oriented understanding of success or of the corresponding obligation. As with the lawyer, there is merely an emphasis on trying as long and as hard as possible: on trying, i.e., on acting. It is therefore not surprising that some who interpret the underlying principle of obligation in an act-oriented fashion "cannot appreciate" Gerald Kelly's "fine distinction between omitting an ordinary means and omitting a *useless* ordinary means." The act-oriented principle would make such a distinction not fine but wrong. The act-oriented principle also confirms Robert Cooke's observation that "Medicine is the science of care, not the science of cure. . . ." Since in this interpretation success is a matter of the caring action, the physician must persevere in it even when he foresees a negative final outcome.

Actual situations hardly ever deal with the definition of success and the physician's attendant obligation—or lack thereof—in such splendid isolation. Considerations like those of limited resources, the patient's rights, and his position in the decision-making process complicate them. However, it is clear that even though saving the patient or curing the disease—the successful result—may prove impossible, this impossibility does not free the medical practitioner from his moral obligation to the patient. It *may* do so, but that depends on the situation, on the patient's rights, and above all on the original understanding between the physician and patient. As in any other contractual or quasi-contractual relationship both physician and patient have a duty to clarify that relationship to one another. Many difficulties stem from the fact that no such clarification has ever taken place. In any case, using a negative prognosis as a blanket justification for euthanasia is unjustifiable: The claim that it does runs counter to that view of medical obligation which sees caring (the action itself) rather than curing (the positive outcome) as the criterion of success.

However, problems also arise with respect to the accuracy of the diagnosis that underlies the prognosis. In fact it may be argued that the whole decision process is liable to error. Mistakes do, after all, occur. Those who advocate euthanasia admit this possibility and those who are inveterately opposed to it frequently raise these fears. According to a relatively recent publication of the Voluntary Euthanasia Society of Great Britain, "Clinical decisions are often what one might call a tossup—they depend on estimates of possibility in which the balance is often rather even" and where by consequence the decision has something of a hit-or-miss nature about it. Such estimates, however, can hardly serve as the bases for deciding on life or death. Nor is the contention significant that those who advocate euthanasia consider it admissible only in situations where benefit is more likely than error. For any such calculation of probabilities requires the very certainty of diagnosis and prognosis that does not exist.

The spectre of error haunts not only the diagnostic procedure; it also appears as an attack on the moral basis of any contemplation of euthanasia. The underlying thesis is that the possibility of error entails an obligation not to act. Since this thesis has wide-ranging implications for any sort of action, medical or otherwise, it is important to evaluate it independently.

THE POSSIBILITY OF ERROR

The arguments from fallibility that are directed against euthanasia generally indicate the various medical mistakes that are possible, mention the grave moral risk involved, and conclude that therefore euthanasia must be rejected. The several possible sources of error that face the physician begin with possibly mistaken medical facts and diagnoses. Even if these are correct, however, there is still no one point in the course of a disease that distinguishes itself as the *punctum saliens*. There is, as Karnofsky acknowledges, "just a gradually changing position from functioning to non-functioning, from ambulation to end. If only one point could be found in this changing scene at which the physician could say, 'this is the point at which I determine death shall take place.'" But there is no such point. Therefore, when to make the decision is largely based on "feel" and experience, not to say personal predilection. Further, the presupposition is that the course of the disease is unalterable and that no remission will occur—a negative prognosis. However, spontaneous remissions, unpredictable and inexplicable as they may be to medical science, do occur. What counts as hopeless given the data available at the time of diagnosis and prognosis may become hopeful in light of new treatments or medications. The physician may have been unaware of them or not had access to them. There actually are cases on record where this information gap meant that the attending physician had given up only to find out about a saving treatment after his decision. In most cases there is no way of telling whether or not this is the case. Consequently not only is a particular prognosis subject to error and a function of the physician's social and subcultural milieu, it is also relative to the physician's knowledge at that place and time.

Sheer prudence therefore requires that in most cases the negative prognosis be treated as conditional only. It is then legitimate to ask whether this is sufficiently secure a basis on which to ground a decision in favour of death. Furthermore, the patient himself should have some say in the matter, but may be comatose or otherwise incommunicado. The impossibility of knowing his desires therefore constitutes yet another possible source of error. So may the fact that by and large a physician lacks the training to evaluate on moral grounds whatever data he actually does possess. All of these possible sources of error combine to make the physician's decision less than certain. However, in situations where a person's life is at stake—so the argument goes—there is a moral duty to keep the possibility of error as close to zero as possible. Not engaging in euthanasia accomplishes this. Therefore, (and quite independently of any particular moral premises about human death and life), according to this argument, it is a physician's moral obligation never to recommend euthanasia simply because such a recommendation always involves a higher risk than the refusal to do so. And the same thing holds, mutatis mutandis, for all those who find themselves in the same decision-making capacity as the physician.

Whatever its shortcomings, this argument has a seductive air of reasonableness about it. Of course we want to keep the possibility of error as low as possible, especially since it concerns a matter of life and death. Of course we would choose to refrain from euthanasia if there were a morally safer course of action open to us, one less liable to error. To act in any other way would be to act irresponsibly and hence immorally, and thus failing in our duty. Therefore on these grounds alone we are tempted to agree that euthanasia must be forbidden.

However, like any attempt at seduction, this approach owes its initial success in no small measure to its emotional appeal. That appeal derives at least in part from an incomplete and slanted presentation of the facts. For instance, there is no question that the possibility of misdiagnosis exists and that distinct diagnoses and prognoses for the same case may differ. Indeed, the second opinion has already passed into common parlance as something of a joke. However, considerations of uncertainty and error do not apply to all cases. Frequently there is unanimity and certainty. For example, in the last stages of cancer of the spine the question of a mistaken diagnosis simply does not arise. In these cases, it may be argued, death would be a release from an unbearable mode of existence—particularly when pain-killing medicaments in life-sustaining doses begin to fail. Here the physician is faced with only three choices: to refrain from administering doses that will hasten or bring death and thereby to leave the pain; to deaden the pain with sufficiently large doses and thereby to hasten death; or, finally, to kill outright. In the end— so the reply could continue—acceptance of the first alternative amounts to condemning the patient to a protracted and hideous but in any case inevitable death by torture (since the means to end the foreknown pain is there—death—the procedure is torture), whereas the second and third alternatives avoid at least this negative preamble to the inevitable demise.

The argument is further slanted in that it draws the boundary of possible cases far too narrowly. As it stands, it addresses itself only to the relatively simple case of one individual in an exceedingly debilitated, painful, and terminal state. But actual cases almost invariably involve an element of triage. Therefore the argument must include such considerations as the socioeconomic and psychological significance of a given patient's survival and also deal with the issue of rights. Furthermore, if the possibility of error in a crucial capacity obliges one not to act then triage contexts would pose an insoluble moral dilemma. In these cases not to engage in selection is still to choose, namely, death for all.

Moral situations that project an air of paradox frequently indicate not genuine difficulty but misunderstanding. May that not be the case here? The physician's possible (or inevitable) medical ignorance and hence error that are used in the argument to preclude any decision in favour of euthanasia can be ameliorated by something known as a responsible consultative process: referring to experts when the situation is not clear. Not only does the physician have the duty to avail himself of this possibility, but the patient also has a similar duty: to provide something like a "living will" in case illness makes him effectively incommunicado. The patient—and in fact any individual—should take this responsibility seriously and realize that his indicated wishes may be used by others and taken to express his real intent. Indeed, those who become aware of this intent are not only morally entitled but duty-bound to take such an expression seriously. Therefore if the patient has fulfilled his duty the physician will know the patient's wishes. Of course error may occur, or the patient may change his mind. But whatever the emotional impact of these possibilities, the moral course of action is clear: A moral agent must bear the consequences of his actions, uncomfortable as at times that may be. This applies to the physician as well as to the patient. Therefore, where the possibility of error lies at the heart of the consideration the onus to minimize it is on both. But it is not an onus *not* to act.

Further, a great deal of the reasonableness of the initial considerations derives from what could be called a calculus of errors: if the liability of error is small but finite on the assumption of euthanasia but drops to zero when euthanasia is ruled out as a possible course of action, reason demands that we adopt the second course. However, at least two considerations nullify this reasoning. The possibility that life could be sheer torture is the first, and must be weighed against the possible error. The second is the impossibility of acting only when consequences are clear and the possibility for error is zero (which is the underlying maxim). For there are no such alternatives. No walk of life, no real situation and no moral problem is so clear and unambiguous. Furthermore, any decision must be based on the available data, faulty and incomplete though they may be, and not on what could be known if the situation were different. If one has made a decision in good faith and to the best of his ability, then all the relevant moral requirements have been met. The decision that results will be morally blameless even though it may eventually be shown to have been wrong or to have been based on faulty or incomplete data. The rule of acting only when consequences are clear also breaks down because it poses an impossible dilemma. Not to act—as when consequences are *not* clear—is to act (think of triage, or the drowning man from whom one withholds aid), and one can err either way. The goal of zero possibility of error therefore becomes impossible.

In the context of euthanasia this means that the physician, having deliberated in good faith and using the best medical data then available, and having examined the situation as carefully as he can, is not merely free but duty-bound to act on his conclusion. Subsequent new (and contrary) data will not change the moral correctness of his action nor detract from his previous duty to act. They will merely mean that it would not be his duty to act so *now*. For *then* he did all that under the circumstances it was possible and reasonable for him to do. One cannot have a duty to do more than what is possible.

To sum up: Any decision process is constrained by the limitations of its present situation. It is impossible to transcend these limits. The considered decision, not made precipitately or foolishly, carries moral obligation. Of course, given new information, the decision might change. Also if the decision should turn out to have been wrong, the decision maker would be profoundly sorry. He would not however be morally guilty. Guilt would result only if the decision was not made in accordance with the preceding parameters. An action in accordance with these, however, is an action in fulfilment of a duty; and one cannot ever become morally guilty by performing a duty.

CONCLUSION

The distinctions between active and passive euthanasia and direct and indirect euthanasia, although perhaps of psychological relevance and physiological significance, are essentially irrelevant from a moral point of view. They do not distinguish what is an act of euthanasia from what is not an act of euthanasia nor do they alter the moral evaluation of the act as it would otherwise obtain.

The question of success or failure in achieving a particular result is not always a relevant consideration when evaluating whether or not there is a duty to engage in the act in the first instance. In some cases performing the act itself constitutes the fulfilment of a duty. Therefore, unless carefully defined and distinguished for a given context, the notion of success is hopelessly ambiguous between an outcome-oriented and an act-oriented interpretation. Consequently, it cannot be claimed that if a successful outcome is ruled out there is no obligation to initiate or continue medical intervention.

The possibility of being mistaken is a universal aspect of the human condition. Therefore fallibility is present in any decision-making context. However, we do have the duty to proceed within the given context in good faith and to the best of our ability. Consequently the mere factor of fallibility does not detract from the obligatoriness of a given course of action if reasonable deliberation should present it as obligatory in the first place.

It is illogical to legitimize what would otherwise be a morally unacceptable act by pointing to the preponderance of good over evil that the act produces and by emphasizing that the undesirable part is unintended. In other words, the doctrine of double effect fails because it is incoherent.

These results do not in any way imply that euthanasia is morally acceptable or, for that matter, morally unacceptable. All they show is that those argumentative approaches that are intended to show that euthanasia is morally good or evil are logically unacceptable, whatever their emotional and historical associations. For the moral status of an act of euthanasia must be evaluated on moral grounds. The following chapters will do so.

2

EUTHANASIA AND THE
INDIVIDUAL

An act of euthanasia is not merely the voluntary, intentional causing of death; it is also an act with moral dimensions. To determine this moral status it is necessary to analyze whether the premises of the arguments for and against euthanasia support the conclusions allegedly based on them and whether they are acceptable as moral premises in the first place, keeping in mind that the cited premises are not always the real ones and that moral maxims sometimes look different in isolation from how they appear in the context of an argument. Among the many arguments for and against euthanasia, the quality of the person's individual life figures prominently.

PAIN AND SUFFERING

With few exceptions (one being Plato's argument from congenital deformity in the *Republic*), arguments in favour of euthanasia are of fairly recent vintage. This is not surprising. Until approximately the turn of the century medical technology was not sufficiently sophisticated for the physician to keep a seriously ill, debilitated, or suffering individual alive to the point where the question of death in order to preserve dignity or preclude what amounted to torture presented any real choice. Death came, and there was little the attendant physician could do about it but give psychological aid and comfort and to try and ease the pain. When Francis Bacon wrote in the *Advancement of Learning*, "we esteem it the office of a physician to mitigate the pains and tortures of diseases, as well as to restore health; and this not only when such a mitigation . . . may conduce to recovery, but also, when there being no farther hopes of recovery, it can only serve to make the passage out of life more calm and easy" he very clearly expressed the traditional situation of the physician. As to those rare cases in which an early end was not to be expected, the prevailing religious rejection of euthanasia as murder served as an effective brake to any attempt to consider euthanasia seriously, let alone implement it as a matter of common practice. Nor should the import of the then current interpretation of the Hippocratic oath be underestimated: Rightly or wrongly, the oath was construed to mean that a physician had the duty never to take a life but always to attempt to preserve it.

Increasing pharmacological sophistication and the advent of intensive mechanically assisted medical care together with the development of new medical techniques have changed all this. Not only can a seriously debilitated, mortally ill individual be kept alive longer than before, but many more people are actually being so sustained. Consequently, problems of pain and suffering, which previously were not socially significant but could be handled on an individual basis, have outstripped the resources of the individual physician, who may well find himself increasingly faced with being able to keep a person alive but only in terrible, unending, and irremediable agony or indignity, or at the price of frequent, debilitating, and unquenchable pain.

Is such a life worth it? At least some have argued that it is not: that when life can be expected to be fraught with agony and suffering, euthanasia is preferable. One aspect of this stance is expressed by S. Gorovitz in a collection of essays entitled *Moral Problems in Medicine:*

There are two different sorts of conditions the presence of which may lead us to judge lives as being of such poor quality that it is questionable whether they are worth living, and hence, worth retrieving. The first is the *pain criterion*: if a life is devoid of any reasonable hope of happiness because of an incapacitating, misery-inducing condition, then the individual in question may want to cease living. Uncontrollable suffering seems at least to call into question the value of the suffering life.

Nor is this statement an isolated instance. Preston Williams suggests in his *Ethical Issues in Biology and Medicine* that life per se is not the highest good; that there are limits to pain and suffering which, when overstepped, if not require then at least permit the patient or physician to choose the course of death. R. H. Williams argues, "Our goal should not be to prolong every life as long as possible. . . . We must consider whether such a prolongation leads to happiness or to great physical and mental suffering for the patient and others." Nor is this stance confined to an essentially medical context. Philosophers like Marvin Kohl have talked about a prima facie duty to kill as a direct consequence of the absolute duty of kindness; and Hugh Trowell states that "voluntary euthanasia rests on a basic human right—the right to die if death is the only release from suffering." Even theologians have entered the debate on the side of euthanasia. Thus W. R. Inge, addressing himself to the situation of someone in great and irremediable suffering, states, "I do not think that we can assume that God willed the prolongation of torture for the benefit of the soul of the sufferer," and others like Paul Ramsey and even Pope Pius XII agree. How else can one understand the former's position that sometimes it is immoral to do more than *only* care for—i.e., alleviate the pain of—the terminally suffering or more than make for Bacon's "fair and easy passage"; or the latter's statement that "extra-ordinary" means—those that "involve . . . a grave burden for oneself"—need not be employed because that "would be too burdensome for most men and would render the attainment of the higher, more important good too difficult."

At the same time this sort of reasoning has not gone unopposed, particularly in the religious sphere. Condoning euthanasia to avoid pain and suffering stands in flagrant opposition to the historical position defended by St. Augustine, who on several occasions roundly rejected the choice of death as morally and theologically wicked, against God's dictates and his plan for the universe. His reasoning was that God has determined matters in such a way that he will turn evil, whether sin or suffering, into good. Even though to our limited gaze a particular life may appear to be no more than a sadistically prolonged existence of incredible and pointless agony, this too has its ultimate role to play. It is not our place to interfere, especially not by contravening God's explicit command not to kill. As he put it in words that were to become fundamental to the development of the doctrine of evil of later Christendom, "That which suffers objects, as it were, to being different from the way it was, because it was something good. But when it is constrained towards the better, its pain is fruitful"; and as he stated in his *City of God*,

Divine providence admonishes us not to misinterpret things foolishly, but to investigate their utility with care; and where our mental capacity or infirmity is at fault, still to believe that there is a utility though hidden . . . . For this concealment of the utility of things itself is either an exercise of our humility or a levelling of our pride; for no nature . . . is evil.

Essentially the same sentiments were echoed by St. Thomas Aquinas in his *Summa Theologiae*:

A particular provider excludes as far as he can all defects from what is subject to his care, whereas one who provides universally allows some little defect to remain lest the good of the whole should be hindered. Therefore corruption and defects in natural things are said to be contrary to some particular nature, but are in keeping with the plan of a universal nature

in that the defect in one thing yields to the good of another. . . . Therefore since God provides universally for all beings, it is part of his providence to allow certain defects in particular effects in order that the perfect
good of the universe may not be curtailed.

In short, both St. Augustine and St. Thomas Aquinas have maintained
that even pain and suffering have purposes and functions and cannot—
indeed, must not—be absent from a perfect creation.

This sort of position is not a mere historical curiosity. Contemporary
theologians have argued to the same effect. Thus Father G. H. Joyce in his
Principles of Natural Theology writes:

One reason plainly why God permits suffering is that man may rise to
a height of heroism which would otherwise have been beyond his
scope. . . . It may be asked whether the Creator could not have brought
man to perfection without the use of suffering. Most certainly he could
have conferred upon him a similar degree of virtue without requiring any
effort on his part. Yet it is easy to see that there is a special value attaching
to a conquest of difficulties such as man's actual demands, and that in
God's eyes this may well be an adequate reason for assigning this life to
us in preference to another. . . .[Furthermore] pain has value in respect
to the next life, but also in respect to this. The advance of scientific
discovery, the gradual improvement of the organization of the community,
the growth of material civilization are due in no small degree to the
stimulus afforded by pain.

Joyce continues, "Just as the human artist has in view the beauty of his
composition as a whole not making it his aim to give each several part
the highest degree of brilliancy, but that measure of adornment which
most contributes to the combined effect, so it is with God." In his article
"Good and Evil" in the *Encyclopedia of Religion and Ethics*, W. D. Niven
agrees: "Physical evil has been the good which has impelled man to more
of those achievements which have made the history of man so wonderful."
In short, the evil of pain and suffering is said to be planned by God for
educational and aesthetic reasons. Even Helmut Thielicke has argued
that while

. . . on the one hand, it is merely part of man's nature to combat suffering,
and in this respect to protect against the natural processes which impose
this suffering on us . . . on the other hand, we are also confronted with
the fact that this suffering could be ordained for us. It could be part
and parcel of our very destiny. What would humanity be if suffering were
to be totally eliminated and we knew nothing but the absurd happiness
of dull lemurs? . . . For pain exercises not only a negative function in our
life but also a creative function whereby it helps us to become what we are
supposed to be.

Sullivan has straight-out characterized pain and suffering as "almost the greatest gift of God's law." The Anglican Church in its pamphlet *On Dying Well* states that"the value of human life does not consist simply of a scale of pleasure over pain" that "Suffering or exposure to what is beyond our voluntary control . . . is part of the pattern of becoming human."

The notion of suffering and pain has also been closely connected with the achievement of moral stature outside of the religious context—with the acquisition of what could be called the moral virtues of perseverance, compassion, patience. These, so it is argued, are also human potentials and are just as much worth developing as all others. Euthanasia would deprive the individual of the opportunity of realizing these possibilities and thus stultify his moral development. As Jose Ortega y Gasset has put it,

Not only is it the case that many of the higher values are constituted in large measure by the difficulty of achievement, but also the more important forms of value—and, perhaps, in the last analysis, all values—are not of the competitive sort, such that they can be attained by some person only if others are deprived of them.

Instead they involve personal difficulties, sacrifice, and suffering in order to attain their full flower. This, we are told, holds not only for the possible euthanasia candidate but also for those who, either as onlookers or as participants in the support drama, might wish to impose euthanasia. Their duty of self-realization also militates against such action because, as Errol E. Harris points out,

. . . it must never be forgotten that among the capacities and values to be realized, the most important are moral potentialities and values, and these include the virtues of compassion and devotion to the welfare of others. Consequently, those who devote themselves to the care of the incapacitated may by so doing be realizing in themselves greater values than they would if they applied their talents to more selfish pursuits.

Furthermore, as *On Dying Well* maintains, "The value of human life does not depend only on its capacity to give"; taking, i.e., giving others the opportunity to help, is also vital. To commit euthanasia, whatever else may be the case, would therefore contravene the duty of moral development and self-realization in both the patient and those caring for him.

Thus both sides of the issue claim a whole range of arguments and a variety of individual positions. Which particular point of view (if any) is defensible and which particular argument (if any) is correct? Several standard replies could be made to the religiously motivated arguments against euthanasia. For instance, to the thesis that pain and suffering have a teaching function and allow the sufferer to rise to heights otherwise unattainable it could be retorted that this has something morally repugnant about it. It is simply incredible to consider agony and undignified, even mindless suffering a deliberate means whereby an omniscient, omnipotent, and omnibenevolent deity wishes to develop virtue in either sufferer or onlooker. That reasoning—so the reply could continue—may have been at home in a religious climate that balanced the evil of sin with the beauty of punishment, which maintained that the suffering of children and infants was designed (at least in part) to teach us a moral lesson, and that insisted that the bliss of the saved in heaven is augmented by the spectacle of the suffering of the damned. Credible only in a theologically and morally barbarous age, this is out of place in the today's theologically responsible and mature context. The universe is not a better place because through agony and suffering people acquire such virtues as fortitude, perseverance, and compassion. It would be better if there were no need for them in the first place. Nor is it at all clear that the evil of pain and suffering is necessary in order for man to become morally good. There are sufficient other opportunities.

As to the aesthetic consideration of a balanced whole, if taken seriously, that would subordinate moral considerations to the principles of aesthetics —a perversion of the true state of affairs. Furthermore, it is true that if the universe must involve situations without remedy then in order for it to be perfect it is better that man be able to rise to the heights of virtue. But there always are remedies. For instance, we can always refuse to prolong such agony by refraining from medical intervention and by making the demise as rapid and easy as possible.

In other words, a strong contingent of modern-day theologians would reply that the virtues enumerated, though indeed virtues, do not require for their realization the sort of continued agony which would otherwise call for euthanasia. To insist that they do, they would argue, is to confuse the ability to rise to those heights with the necessity of doing so.

Furthermore, to hold that God permits pain and suffering so that man may become morally good is to reduce the refusal to accept euthanasia to a business proposition: If we gather enough heavenly credits by suffering or by acquiring a certain attitude towards suffering, then after death we will be rewarded by God. However, religion is not a business proposition. Anything that would reduce it to such must be rejected.

Finally and pragmatically, accepting and implementing this stance consistently could result in reluctance or even refusal to alleviate any pain and suffering, terminal or otherwise. After all—so it could be argued— if pain and suffering, disease and corruption, debility and morbidity all have their place in the grand design, what right have we to interfere? Ever? (Unless, of course, our interference is also part of God's plan, in which case the whole position becomes circular.) The crisis of consistency resulting from this reasoning would ramify throughout the whole sphere of religiously determined action; for it is highly doubtful that physicians would stop practising and relief organizations stop helping out of the conviction that man should be virtuous.

At the same time the argument could also be turned around. When contemporary theologians like Inge and Pope Pius XII, aware of these ramifications, attempt to ameliorate the traditional stance by claiming that in certain instances euthanasia is permissible, the traditional anti-euthanasiast may point out that the ultimate logical consequence of this is a denial of the need of suffering for God's plan. And this in turn raises a series of difficult questions: What happens to the reason for *any* continuation of suffering? If the Judaeo-Christian belief in the divine plan can be abandoned in order to allow people to die so as not to lengthen their pain and suffering, why not advocate outright killing if that should be the only way to achieve this end? Why, as most contemporary theologians who are prepared to move this way maintain, should only passive euthanasia be acceptable and not active euthanasia as well? If not to intervene (e.g., extend a helping hand to a drowning person) affects the outcome as much as intervening would, there is no morally significant difference between the two sorts of cases.

Further objections, this time from outside of the framework of religious assumptions, have been raised explicitly since the time of Hume: What reason is there to accept the hypothesis of a divine plan in the first place? Of a plan, moreover, that permits and even necessitates pain and suffering and that brands as evil the ultimate attempt to alleviate that suffering when all else fails? Surely—so it is argued—any system of beliefs that prevents us from alleviating suffering in the only way possible is by that very token morally objectionable and must be abandoned. Therefore, the arguments that God intends man to develop virtue by suffering are not only unacceptable in themselves; they also throw doubt on the acceptability of the whole religious stance in which they are at home. Perhaps the Manicheans were right after all: Perhaps God, although all good and all knowing, is not all powerful and cannot prevent the evil of suffering. In which case it is morally incumbent on *us* to try.

The religiously associated position on euthanasia in the case of pain and suffering is thus inconsistent and incoherent. Perhaps Thielicke's vacillating stance is the best that can be achieved, given the existing limitations: On the one hand there are God's commands and the divine plan; on the other there are our moral conviction and the duty of kindness. The apparent confrontation is not helped by the essentially transcendental nature of revelation itself.

Arguments against euthanasia that arise outside of the religious sphere and therefore do not depend on revealed premises also encounter difficulties. To begin with Ortega y Gasset's argument for the development of moral virtues as a matter of the self-realization of man. This stance is of respectable parentage. It has its roots in the notions of virtue postulated by Plato and Aristotle. Nevertheless, at the same time the objections raised against the religious stance can also be raised in this connection. Man does indeed have an emotional, feeling side as integral to him as the intellectual and the physiological. It is also true that the development of this side ultimately results in virtues such as compassion, perseverance, and fortitude. However this does not mean that therefore we should refrain from euthanasia. For developing and exercising these virtues depends on the continued existence of agony and suffering. But, it is one thing to argue that *if* such suffering exists then it will allow us to develop these virtues; it is quite another to say that there should be those virtues. Medical literature furnishes enough examples of unbearable situations from which death is the only possible release. Here, to refuse to *grant* euthanasia in the name of virtue would be to refuse to grant release from suffering and insist on what is in effect torture simply in order to be able to develop one's own emotional potential for such virtues as compassion and charity; to refuse to *request* euthanasia solely in order to develop patience and hope would be to glory in an unbearable state solely on the basis of the assumption that it is somehow better, absolutely speaking, to have these virtues than not.

And that is a mistake. Of course compassion, devotion to duty, perseverance, humility, hope, and charity are virtues. But not always, and above all not in an absolute sense. An obviously inappropriate virtue would be compassion for the foiled embezzler, or for the would-be murderer whose concerted efforts to kill have failed. For we must distinguish between two sorts of virtues: absolute and relative. Absolute virtues are those which no morally fully developed and perfect person may be without, no matter what the nature of the world, his own nature, or the vagaries of the circumstances in which he finds himself. They add to the moral quality of the world. A universe which has these virtues in it is better than a universe that does not. The refusal to engage in deception, either to oneself or to others, is one of these virtues, as is the desire to attain as far as possible one's potential as a rational being. Relative virtues, on the other hand, are not such that a morally fully developed and perfect individual must have them, nor is a universe in which there are no such virtues necessarily worse than a universe in which they exist. In fact, quite the opposite may be the case. If there are virtues which can arise only in response to some defect in a universe, then a universe in which there was no such defect and correspondingly no such virtues would still be better than a universe in which those virtues existed because of the inherent defects of the universe itself. The existence of absolute virtues does not require as precondition some defect in the universe, in this case agony and suffering. Therefore being a virtuous person in the absolute sense cannot depend on the existence of agony and suffering. These may be necessary in order to acquire relative virtues—but that does not show that it is better absolutely speaking to have these virtues than not.

The virtues in question—patience, perseverance, hope, compassion—are relative, not absolute. In our apparently imperfect world with its pain and suffering, it is better that they exist than not. But euthanasia is not therefore immoral. For whether absolute or relative, no virtue may require continued suffering by the alleged beneficiaries of the supposedly virtuous acts. Therefore the exercise of other-regarding virtues such as compassion and devotion cannot involve a refusal to grant euthanasia when all other means of relief are impossible. Quite the opposite. The very possession of these relative virtues demands that we grant euthanasia when nothing else will ameliorate the condition. The same holds for patience, forbearance, and perseverance as had by the individual himself. It cannot be a necessary condition of the exercise of these virtues that the debilitating, agonizing, undignified state which makes these relative virtues possible be prolonged. It is just that if nothing can be done to alter the circumstances then it is better that these obtain. But that is a far cry from the contention that their very exercise, no matter what, should include no desire for or decision to terminate through euthanasia the condition that called them forth in the first place.

Consequently, even if there is a duty of self-realization that includes the moral (as well as the intellectual and physical) side of man it still would not follow that euthanasia contravenes that duty. On the contrary: Euthanasia might well be seen as the final test of whether or not a given individual, be he patient or spectator, had attained full moral self-realization. To argue otherwise is to confuse the thesis that *if* suffering exists it is better to have compassion and devotion with the thesis that it is better, absolutely speaking, that there be these virtues *no matter what*. It is also to be confused over what the exercise of these relative virtues entails. While their exercise presupposes the existence of the suffering just indicated, it does not involve its prolongation. If anything, the exercise of compassion would bring about whatever amelioration is possible under the circumstances. Sometimes this will mean euthanasia. In such cases to refuse to engage in euthanasia is actually to be a causal determinant of the prolongation of pain and suffering: It is to *fail* to be virtuous and thereby to become immoral.

Finally, it may also be argued that the whole reasoning involved in the initial moral argument fails on purely logical grounds: It attempts to derive a moral duty from a purely material premise. The mere fact that something has a certain nature in and by itself does not, however, entail any moral consequence, let alone an injunction for or against euthanasia.

But difficulties are not confined to the arguments against euthanasia. Those in favour also have their share. To begin with a purely factual problem, the thesis that sometimes suffering is irremediable except by death is factually mistaken. Medical drugs and techniques exist that can alleviate pain without inducing or hastening death. That is why physicians like Thomas Lohman have stated categorically that "pain must not be fought by means of the death of the patient." The perhaps unavoidable side effects of stupor and even unconsciousness are deemed preferable to murder (though Lohman appears to stop short of this in favour of "passive euthanasia" or accidentally, unavoidably shortening life).

Another questionable assumption is that life is not worth living in great pain and suffering. This argument purports to reflect the sufferers' views. However, research about such patients' attitudes and opinions has shown that, although some do want to die, many do not and continue to value life. F. B. Sumner captures their stance vividly: "One of the most pathetic and curious facts of human existence is the tenacity with which most persons cling to life, however tragic . . . and however painful in the last stages. The patient fights for his life."

The pro-euthanasia argument from pain and suffering is further defective because it assumes that if a pain-filled existence has no value for the person it has no value at all, and euthanasia is therefore appropriate. But one could well argue that there is a difference between something *having* a value and something being of value *to* or having value *for* someone. As it stands, so one could continue, the argument confuses the two and represents as absolute what is only a relative matter. The implication of this, in turn, is still another critique: Unless and until the proponent of the argument from pain and suffering has shown either that life has no absolute value and that whatever value it has reduces to its being valued by someone or that life has an absolute value but that the sort of value it has depends on the pleasure-pain proportion to be found in it, the argument as a whole must be rejected as question-begging, its overwhelming emotional appeal notwithstanding.

Still another logical shortcoming of the argument is that the choice of either agony or death, on which the argument rests, is not complete. There is at least one alternative: Unless the source of pain is located in the brain —an exceedingly rare occurrence—it lies within the power of modern medicine to remove it entirely if necessary by the radical section of the spinal cord or some such surgical intervention. To be sure, the side effects of such a procedure are drastic. But the procedure does away with the pain. Therefore the dichotomy on which the argument rests—either unending agony or death—is not exhaustive, and its conclusion does not follow. To the objection that such a surgical procedure would itself be exceedingly debilitating and that the resultant life, although pain-free, would be of exceptionally low and "worthless" quality, two replies are possible. First, it would still be less radical than euthanasia. Second, what is at issue in the present context are pain and suffering. All other considerations, although perhaps telling in a different context, are irrelevant to this reasoning.

Furthermore, anyone arguing for euthanasia on the basis of pain and suffering must establish three things: that pain and suffering are in fact present; they are not merely relevant but in fact decisive in deciding whether a given life has sufficient value to be worth living; and that the nature and degree of pain and suffering actually present are such as to warrant euthanasia.

The presence of pain is relatively easy to determine. Although in principle no one can experience anyone else's pain, nevertheless we do have practical criteria sufficiently precise and unquestionable to render the whole problem academic.

To show that suffering is a decisive criterion in euthanasia, however, would require two difficult things: a theory about the interrelationship between the value of life and pain, and a precise analysis of the qualities of pain and suffering that would make it possible to quantify them.

Nor is it any easier to show that the nature and degree of suffering actually present are sufficient to warrant euthanasia. This requirement not only presupposes that suffering exists and that the requisite theory, analysis, and quantification are provided, but it also requires that euthanasia be one of the options. Furthermore, not only is there the question of whether the quality and quantity of the pain are indeed unbearable in a given context—whatever that may mean—there is also the question of the likelihood of a cure. Any answer, however, involves an ineluctable element of prognostication. And while admittedly it may be too much to ask for absolute certainty in a given case, it may nevertheless be argued that the element of uncertainty that does obtain, when coupled with the other difficulties already mentioned, is sufficient to undermine the cogency of the reasoning as a whole.

That leaves the argument from the duty of kindness. Some, for instance Marvin Kohl, have argued that euthanasia is an obligation necessitated (under certain circumstances) by that very duty. Others, for example H. T. Engelhardt, even speak of "the injury of continued existence."

But, it can be argued that this position is logically absurd. An analogy will make this clear: Suppose that my car has been performing quite badly, running inefficiently, burning a lot of oil, and polluting the air. Suppose further that I go to a mechanic and ask him to correct this undesirable state of affairs. He then has two options: He can wreck the car, thus getting rid of the inefficiency and pollution; or he can rebore the cylinders, replace the pistons, and tune the engine. Both choices would eliminate the problem, but only the second would be acceptable. The first would be a gross misunderstanding of the injunction to correct the state of affairs. If it should turn out that the second option cannot remedy the situation, a new and separate command to wreck the car would be required before the mechanic could claim to have been entitled—enjoined —to wreck it.

The relevance of this analogy to the problem of euthanasia is this: We are said to have the duty of kindness. Applied to the present context, this is supposed to mean that we have the duty to correct (ameliorate) the undesirable state of pain and suffering. However, just as the mechanic's obligation to correct the fault in the car is not the obligation to remove the car itself from the scene, so the obligation to remove the objectionable situation of pain and suffering is not the obligation to remove the individual who is in pain and suffering. However, to construe the general duty of kindness as entailing the obligation to engage in euthanasia is to construe that general duty in precisely this way—and thus to misconstrue it.

The same point can be put more explicitly as follows: The duty to kindness does not exist in a vacuum. It is owed *to* a person; in this case the patient. However, the duty to remove his suffering is different from the duty to remove the patient himself. The latter, if it is a duty at all, is a duty *about* him. Therefore it is logically illegitimate to argue that if it is impossible for us to fulfil the duty to remove a person's suffering then we have the duty to do something else—namely, to kill him. It may be that there is such a duty, but if so it is not entailed by the duty of kindness. Certainly it is logically distinct from the duty to remove pain and suffering. To remove an experience of an individual and to remove the individual himself are entirely different things.

Finally, we have not even raised the host of issues centering around the question of decision-making power. Whose word is the last authority? The patient's? The physician's? Society's? Even without these further questions, however, it is clear that considerations of pain and suffering, if intended to establish that euthanasia is morally acceptable, are not decisive.

This is not to say that those arguments which are intended to show that pain and suffering are, if not irrelevant to the question of euthanasia, then at least something that must simply be borne until the unassisted end, fare any better. There is something inherently repugnant about torturing people to death. By the same token, there is something morally objectionable about allowing people to die in prolonged agony or even being a cause of the prolonging of their torture. At least this is so if the previous analysis of the nature of acts is correct. For according to that analysis, to allow people to die in torture without taking whatever steps are possible to end that torture is to be a causal determinant of that state of torture itself. Of course, if there are moral principles that demand such a course of action then we should simply be faced with a duty, and that would settle the matter. But logical fairness forces us to contend that unless and until such fundamental principles are established the duty to refrain from euthanasia does not follow.

Another problem has not even been hinted at: How do we know that there are duties (in the morally relevant sense of that term) in the first place? Those in favour of euthanasia could simply argue that they prefer to die rather than to subsist in lingering suffering and agony, and those who oppose them could simply argue that they prefer the opposite. That, however, would not be a moral confrontation. It would be one of preference. Nor would it be possible for either side to argue that the other is wrong. They could merely say that they disagree in their preferences. Moral confrontation involves the notions of obligation and duty. Unless these are clarified, the whole dispute is logically up in the air.

DEATH AND DIGNITY

The fear not merely of death but of vegetating encrusted with tubes, respirator, and pacemaker, drugged into stupor or mindlessness and nevertheless alive, sometimes agonizingly so—in short, the fear of ending in a "living death"—has made many converts to the cause of euthanasia. Their position can be summed up in a single cry: Death with dignity! The argument from dignity is standard in most pro-euthanasia legislative draft proposals, is adduced by theologians and physicians alike, and is brought forward as an extenuating circumstance by barristers intent on defending their clients from a charge of murder. The following excerpt from Veatch's recent draft proposal puts the thrust of these considerations quite clearly:

To my family, my physician, my clergyman, my lawyer: If the time comes when I can no longer take part in decisions for my own future, let this statement stand as a testament of my wishes: If there is no reasonable expectation of my recovery from physical or mental disability, I, ———— , request that I be allowed to die and not be kept alive by artificial means or heroic measures. Death is as much a reality as birth, growth, maturity and old age—it is the one certainty. *I do not fear death as much as I fear the indignity of deterioration, dependence and hopeless pain.* I ask that medication be mercifully administered to me for terminal suffering even if it hastens the moment of death.

Undeniably there appears to be something "undignified" about dying the slow death of a "human vegetable." But can dignity be a criterion for death? For dignity is a social concept that differs from society to society, from culture to culture, and even from era to era within the same culture. Therefore what is called undignified must be understood to be so with respect to a particular context and time.

But even this is insufficient. What constitutes an indignity even in the same place and time may be debatable. This is so at the present time. For opposed to the evaluation of a "living death" as "undignified" is Regier's stance, which also enjoys wide acceptance. As she quotes Judge Muir, "Continuation of medical treatment, in whatever form, where its goal is the sustenance of life, is not something degrading, arbitrarily inflicted, unacceptable in contemporary society or unnecessary." Therefore, the claim that an indignity is involved in attempting to keep someone alive at all costs ultimately turns out to be a personal judgment. But whose? The patient's? He may be unable to communicate or even clearly evaluate his position. The patient before he reaches this state, as the living will itself suggests? That conjures up the spectre of fallibility, of mental incompetence at the time of writing, and of a different evaluation from the patient were he able to respond again. Those involved in a supportive capacity or mere onlookers? That of course is the real possibility hinted at by Judge Muir in the preceding passage: Those around the patient may find their sensibilities violated and unconsciously project their attitudes onto the patient. As Ramsey points out, "The permanent and deeply unconscious person is, so far as can be known, not suffering at all. An argument that he should be treated 'mercifully' by being allowed to die or by being killed is misplaced. It is only the suffering of the relatives that should be relieved." In which case the whole argument reduces to the question of the convenience and emotional equilibrium of others. The dignity of the patient has become irrelevant.

What dignity amounts to in the first place, then, and whose dignity is at stake are not at all clear. Therefore, before we can accept the claim that someone in an undignified, irremediable medical condition has the right to die, we require what is so far missing: a definition of dignity that does not reduce to pleasure or personal whim, as well as proof that dignity has moral dimensions.

Finally, the appeal to dignity itself is inconsistent. In the living will, for instance, death is characterized as a reality of the universe like birth growth, maturity, and old age and therefore something that cannot and should not be avoided at all cost. The attempt to save life, on the other hand, is branded as unnatural. However, if old age is a reality so are the infirmities of old age—senile dementia, loss of physical faculties, and increased dependence on others. If death is a reality, so is the desire for life. It, like aging, is part of our genetically determined make-up and is as natural or "real" as the process of growth and maturation. Therefore if by "real" is meant "natural"—as the examples proffered seem to indicate —then to wish for death, precisely because it would go against what is natural *in that very sense*, would also be unrealistic. In other words, if the watchword is "dignity" and "dignity" means "natural" or "real" this argument does not stand. The use of our intellect is also "realistic" since it too is an inborn function. Why then, characterize as unrealistic the exercise of that capacity to extend the limit of life?

However, to argue thus is to invite the charge of unfairness. The real point of the argument is that to continue to fight against odds which from the beginning are known to be hopeless is foolhardy, that to insist on doing so in the face of pain and indignity is unrealistic and sadistic. To this there is only one reply: This position may well be true—always supposing that the notion of dignity has been defined satisfactorily and that there is a moral connection between dignity and the right to death—but only as a general principle. In order to be relevant in practice we require that here and now, for this individual under these circumstances, the relevant criteria of indignity and hopelessness are met. This constitutes a bar to any generalization from one situation to another. No rules can be laid down; we must look and see.

SENESCENCE

Death with dignity is frequently associated with the notion of age. It conjures up the image of an older person at the end of his life subjected to what are described as undignified conditions in order to save his life. In some quarters, therefore, age has become the focus of a train of reasoning in favour of euthanasia that involves considerations of triage, of the dignity of the patient, the quality of his life, his mental state, and even his social usefulness.

Nevertheless, sometimes age is also considered by itself. The reasoning then goes something like this: Once a human being has passed the third decade of his life, a gradual but inexorable and irreversible aging process sets in. Physiologically this evinces itself only slightly in the beginning, but as time goes on the deterioration becomes cumulative until around age sixty-five it becomes noticeable. Impairment of memory, shortened attention span, emotional instability, and a general difficulty in learning begin to manifest themselves as a result of the increasing deterioration of the brain; the function of the cardiovascular system is impaired, shortness of breath and a general lack of stamina predominate, and digestive difficulties set in—to say nothing of an increasing loss of overall sensory acuity. In short, a general functional discapacity of the system begins to manifest itself. All these functional impairments combine to interfere with the quality of the person's life, impose a burden on a society to which he no longer contributes, and in extreme cases result in such an undignified infantile regression or even disconsciousness that we may wonder whether we are still dealing with a person. The morally correct procedure is to opt for euthanasia in the medically relevant cases, if not actively then at least passively by refusing to engage in medical intervention to prolong life. Better for the individual to die with dignity than to continue as a burden to himself and others. If there should be such a scarcity of medical resources that selection for treatment becomes an issue, then these aged should have a low priority. Not only is the likelihood of their future contribution to society small, but also they "have already lived."

Logically speaking, this argument is quite complex. It includes not only the medical factors involved in senescence itself but also social associations and considerations of triage. Some of these—claims of dignity, emotional and mental acumen and stability, as well as the various social considerations—are concepts influenced by culture. Our society places a premium on youth and fitness; Daniel Maguire's observation with respect to an expressed desire by old people in our culture is therefore particularly penetrating: "Perhaps the desire for death is due not so much to the illness [or, we might add, the factor of senescence itself] as it is to the dehumanized atmosphere that others have created." If our approach and outlook towards the aged were different, perhaps the "tiredness" of the old and debilitated would not be a reason for voluntary euthanasia. Aside from this however, there is the question whether the purely medical phenomenon of aging with its psychological and physiological ramifications constitutes a necessary or sufficient ground for euthanasia.

There is here no hard and fast answer. It all depends on the precise facts of the situation as well as on the moral premises used to evaluate these facts.

This last statement focuses on what is probably one of the most important things to keep in mind in any discussion of euthanasia: If by "reason" is meant a morally inclining or imperative onus, then in and by themselves there are no medical reasons for or against euthanasia at all. Medical considerations, like any other factual data, are just that: wholly factual. Like the deliberations of a plumber, a shopkeeper, or a demolition expert, those of a physician deal with what is and is not the case; they tell us what we must do and what we must refrain from doing, to achieve certain results. In short, they are descriptive, not prescriptive. They cannot and do not tell us what ought and ought not to be done in any absolutely imperative and above all moral sense. Moral commands, however, do precisely that. They are injunctions that tell us what is morally right or wrong, what is obligatory, allowed, or proscribed. They hold independently of our desires and wishes (although these are not irrelevant to the decision). No practical art or discipline concerned with purely factual matters can supply them. Therefore no matter how correct the various aspects of gerontology in their findings, no matter how justified their conclusions about senility or the various aspects of senescence and the socioeconomic calculations of possible productive return, these are no substitute for moral precepts. Without such precepts these facts remain morally neutral. (It is tempting to argue that physicians might "covenant together" to provide themselves with a set of moral precepts, thus making the medical facts no longer morally neutral. The problem is that their agreement does not make the precepts moral; it merely specifies what behaviour the physicians find acceptable. Whether it is moral is still an open question. Also, even if the precepts were moral ones, they would not have been determined by the physicians in their capacity as physicians but as moral agents concerned about the nature of right and wrong. Their status as physicians, although it undoubtedly supplies them with examples of morally difficult situations, will not confer any greater *moral* urgency on their deliberations than that of any other profession.)

A practical discipline like medicine, then, by its very nature does not provide any moral premises. Are there premises that supply this lack? Premises that deal with the facts of senescence but at the same time contain a moral and therefore prescriptive element? Unquestionably there are. For instance: Whenever an old person becomes a psychological, physiological or financial burden to his family or social grouping, if the medical option presents itself he should be allowed to die. Or: Whenever an old person competes with a young one for access to limited medical resources, the latter should have greater priority since his life will be socially more productive. Or: Whenever an old person's brain has reached such a state of deterioration that he is scarcely aware of who he is or what is going on, then the employment of medical means to save or sustain his life should be interdicted. Or: Whenever the general physiological debility attendant upon senescence has left an individual with an illness from which only protracted and difficult procedures will rescue him, then these need not be attempted and the individual may be allowed to die.

However, two things quickly become apparent: First, the very same sort of reasoning, mutatis mutandis, could be used to argue in favour of euthanasia for anyone else who finds himself in an analogous state of physiological debility and deterioration. The fact of senescence itself does not appear to play any real role in the decision-making process or, for that matter, in the moral premises necessary for the latter (the second premise possibly excepted). But this brings in the second point: The purely medical aspect of senescence has dropped out of the picture as having moral relevance even in that case in which it is mentioned. Instead it seems to have been reduced to a mere ad hoc device for identifying the specific group to which the actual criteria themselves are intended to apply. These criteria have nothing to do with age at all. Instead they involve utility and social significance. Consequently, not only does the use of senescence (age) as a criterion still require justification, but also the principles of utility and social significance which now emerge as the real moral criteria still have to be spelled out and defended.

Not only that: who is to apply these moral criteria? The physician's medical expertise, which obviously qualifies him to make decisions based on medical criteria like senescence, does not guarantee expertise in moral matters. He is competent to decide who is senescent and who is not; but he is not thereby competent to decide whether or not this has moral relevance and, if so, of what sort and how much. Nor can the fact of his medical expertise be allowed to obscure the possible relevance of the patient's own determinations or of society in general. Who is to decide?

These and analogous considerations suggest that senescence does not constitute the real reason in favour of euthanasia, either in itself or in the general context of the other so-called medical indications. Instead the contention that those who are not young, productive, and stable should be euthanatized—allowed to die—seems to be based on the essentially utilitarian premise of the greatest good for the greatest number of people. But this premise is applicable not only in the case of senescence. Consistency requires that if it is applied at all it be so in all cases that meet the moral conditions contained in it. Of course, age itself *could* become the major moral factor. But unless the moral relevance of age is somehow shown this remains a flagrantly ad hoc and discriminating premise. The case for euthanasia in the event of moribund senescence must therefore be made on some other basis. That is why those impassioned pleas for euthanasia for the aged whom Joseph Fletcher describes as comatose and "betubed and sedated and aerated and glucosed and *non compos mentis*," depend for whatever logical cogency they have not on the fact that these are *old* people but on the fact that these are *people* who are betubed and sedated. . . . Only when it is assumed that *people* in general should be killed (allowed to die) under such circumstances and for the reasons offered does the conclusion apply to the senescent as well. Anything else would be an arbitrary stipulation to the effect that under certain conditions a specific age group constitutes "surplus population."

At the same time this conclusion undeniably raises problems, especially in situations of triage. Suppose that there is a limited amount of medical resources insufficient to save or sustain two (or more) individuals but sufficient for only one; suppose further that all factors such as prognosis for recovery and quality of life (in whatever appropriate sense this may be understood) are even; and suppose, finally, that there is a significant age difference between the competitors for these resources, e.g., the one patient is 15, the other 75. Is it not reasonable to give the resources to the former? And does this not show that age per se is a morally relevant factor after all and that an argument from senescence may, under certain circumstances, be morally valid?

To be blunt, the answer is no. It is not age that is telling here but the considerations tacitly associated with age: duties and obligations owed to others in the community; duties and obligations owed by others to them; even duties and obligations with respect to each other as members of the same community; prognosis of future contribution to the society; fairness; and so on. These frequently result in a decision in favour of the younger individual and against the senescent—but not always and because he is younger. Therefore even these considerations drawn from actual situations of ordinary life do not support the criterion of senescence. If anything, they show that age as such is a morally irrelevant factor in these decisions and that the real basis lies elsewhere. Of course, this is not to say that those who are in a decision-making position do not sometimes appeal to it; but it is to show that if and when they do they are morally wrong.

BRAIN FUNCTION

One of the factors that cropped up several times in the preceding considerations was that of the deterioration of the brain functions of a senescent individual to such a degree that "we may wonder whether we are still dealing with a person." As a matter of practical concern, this sort of consideration is accorded great weight in decisions for or against euthanasia. In some quarters it is even seen as *the* moral determinant of the quality of life. For—so the reasoning seems to run—if such a nadir of mental faculties has been reached that the life in question "scarcely seems human to us at all," as Gorovitz says, then, surely an absolute low point in the quality of life has been reached as well. Here if anywhere qualitative considerations seem to speak for euthanasia. Furthermore, unlike age, such a criterion is said to avoid arbitrary discrimination. It would apply to all individuals alike, irrespective of age, sex, colour, creed, or socioeconomic position. Also, so the argument continues, it would have the considerable advantage of being a morally relevant criterion, for there is no properly "human life" without mental function. But where there is no "human life" there is no person; and where there is no person the question of euthanasia as a serious moral issue cannot even be raised. (This is not to say that there is no such thing as a moral or immoral act towards animals.) Consequently, complete brain dysfunction would constitute the ultimate criterion under the rubric of "quality of life."

The reasoning just sketched may be correct. As a matter of fact I believe that, suitably amended and fleshed out, it is. But it raises questions that are at the very heart of the ethics of euthanasia. For, investigating the interrelationship (if any) between euthanasia and the quality of life requires not only a discussion of the nature of personhood—of what it is to be a person from an ethical viewpoint in relation to physiological criteria and psychological manifestations—it also involves the topic of duties and rights: When and under what conditions do these attach to an individual? Do they attach to human beings as such? To human beings who are persons? Absolutely speaking or only relative to certain circumstances? The list of questions could go on. I shall therefore devote a separate discussion to these crucial issues a little later and simply conclude the present chapter with a brief look at the notion of quality of life itself.

THE QUALITY OF LIFE

The arguments in this chapter have all claimed more or less directly that quality of life either is or is not a determining criterion for euthanasia. In so doing, they have all been guilty of assuming that the meaning of the central phrase, "quality of life," is transparent and well-known, requiring neither definition nor clarification. But this is not true. What "quality of life" means depends on one's socioeconomic and cultural milieu. The fact of this unclarity, however, may be exploited in a very general argument against advocating euthanasia on a qualitative basis.

The argument would proceed something like this: Advocating euthanasia because life is not worth living requires specifying precisely what aspects of life are to be included in the analysis and the degree of deterioration that is considered permissible before euthanasia is indicated. It also necessitates showing why qualitative considerations should be considered morally telling in the first place. After all, it may be the case that any human life has absolute and intrinsic value, in which case any considerations of quality would be beside the point. Furthermore, even granting the relevance of considerations of the quality of life, there is still the problem of defining and then quantifying these inherently qualitative aspects. Yet even if the concept of quality of life were suitably defined and its elements supplied with a quantitative calculus, and even if life had no absolute value, it would still not follow that someone whose life fell below the cut-off point had the right or duty to euthanasia—or that anyone else had a corresponding duty or right. Any claim to the contrary would involve a logical jump. The only thing that would follow would be that such a life need not be prized—a different thing entirely.

Of course, the shortcomings of the reasoning could be patched up with a suitable premise. But what would that premise be? What is not worth living may be (must be?) destroyed? Clearly this premise is not entirely acceptable as a general maxim. Certainly it needs defence. A premise based on the principle of the greatest good for the greatest number would provide the easiest solution; but that would require a defence of utilitarianism which, if past attempts are anything to go on, may not be an easy task.

Finally, the emotional claim that the refusal to allow euthanasia in cases of interminable suffering and agony is to condemn the individual to a life of sadistically prolonged torture, is quite out of place in any attempt to evaluate the ethics of euthanasia. Emotions and feelings about the matter, although in and by themselves interesting as psychological data, are irrelevant to the enterprise unless their moral significance can somehow be established. Otherwise they must be ignored as deeply felt but unfortunately irrelevant emotional manifestations in a moral dis- cussion. To establish that they are relevant, however, is to show that they are justified—which is to show that euthanasia is (or is not) morally reprehensible; and that is the very point at issue.

At the same time it must be admitted that the case against qualitative considerations is not quite as one-sided as all that. It is true that any argu- ment advocating euthanasia on qualitative grounds must fulfil all the requirements mentioned. It must specify the particular qualitative ele- ments involved and the level of qualitative deterioration at which the euthanasia clause goes into effect. Above all, it must make it possible to measure and thus evaluate the qualitative elements. It is also true that it must still make the transition from the qualitative considerations, which are purely descriptive, to the moral injunctions, which are inherently prescriptive: from "is qualitatively worthless" (negative, insufficient) in some as yet-to-be-specified fashion to "has the right (duty) to kill (be killed)." And what is more, it must do so without confusing what is obvious—a purely psychological phenomenon—with what is moral: a matter of ethics.

However, these considerations can be reversed. They also apply to those arguments that are intended to show that a particular life is worth saving or sustaining because human life per se has absolute value, or because a particular life has not reached a specific nadir, or because it does meet certain qualitative criteria, or because to terminate it would be opportunistic, coldblooded, and cruel. In fact, so far from showing that any particular position on euthanasia is correct, they show that any argument that is based on considerations of the quality of life, whether it be for or against, is logically incomplete until certain lacunae have been filled. What are needed are fundamental, defensible moral premises. Without these we may have statements of preference and inclination, assertions of what is feasible or possible or what it is merely expensive to do; but we shall not have any morally compelling reasons or injunctions on which to base decisions of life and death.

3

EUTHANASIA AND SOCIETY

Man, according to Aristotle, is a rational animal: His nature is not purely intellectual but involves both physical and psychological attributes. Therefore, so Aristotle maintained, full development of the human potential has to include both body and mind, and any sacrifice of the one to the other ultimately stultifies the whole human nature. At the same time Aristotle insisted that because man is also a social animal, the complete realization of his properly human nature cannot occur in isolation but requires a social context.

This tripartite characterization of human nature is as appropriate now as it was then. Man is an *animal*—he is a living organism that is born, grows, and ultimately dies. Man is a *rational* animal—he has self-awareness and cogitative powers, and at least in principle the various aspects of his life are subject to his deliberation and reasoned control. Man is a *social* animal—the control of his abilities is not solely determined by him as an individual but as a member of the social group which shares in developing his personality and ultimately sets the external limits to the realization of his potentials as a human being. As Edgar Bodenheimer points out, "Quite obviously the individual cannot attain the self-realization to which his nature impels him as an isolated being in a social vacuum. Without the framework of a social system affording him opportunities for productive effort he cannot develop his powers to the fullest."

Man's development and fulfilment, then, are ultimately social phenomena. This includes his birth as well as his death. His birth he cannot control, although he can attempt to control the birth of others. His death, however, is subject to direct intervention and determination on his own part. Therefore, the issue of euthanasia can be seen as the issue of control over the individual's death. Ought it to rest with the individual himself or with society? On what basis should it be exercised? Is such control morally right? The concern centres around the nature and legitimacy of such control. Not, of course, in the purely legal sense—although that too is present—but in the moral one. Who is to be the ultimate arbiter?

These questions are more important even than the question of how we should live our lives, for the latter can arise only after it has been determined whether we should live at all. They are also doubly complicated: Not merely because the social context in which they typically arise is itself complex; but because there are two radically distinct vantage-points from which the issue can be approached: either from the point of view of the individual who happens to require a social setting for his existence and development or from the point of view of the social complex as a whole, of which the individual is a member and through which he attains personhood. There is no dearth of arguments about euthanasia that focus on the social outlook. They identify it variously as dangerous to the fabric of society or as a welcome tool of social policy; they focus on the practical dangers inherent in legally sanctioning this extension of society's control over the life of the individual citizen or point to the consequences of allowing the individual himself such decision-making power, they concentrate on the situation's economic and political aspects or comment on its psychological and administrative ramifications. The variations are almost endless.

RADICAL EGOISM

"Moral man," says G. H. Roux "must certainly be granted considerable leeway in deciding on the how's and why's of his life, and likewise, on the use of his body; but we can never condone full autonomy over his body without floundering in the quagmire of radical egoism." This remark seems to object not so much to euthanasia per se as to giving complete control of euthanasia to the individual. The reason for this objection to voluntary or requested euthanasia appears to be both pragmatic, involving the nature of social dynamics in general, and moral, dealing with the value-status of the individual as opposed to that of society.

The social dynamics thesis is this: Society, it is argued, requires for its survival and proper functioning that its members have a coherent, integrated interrelationship. This in turn requires that the individual play a more or less subservient role to society as a whole. Therefore while the individual may be allowed a certain degree of self-determination in his daily affairs (since this does not usually interfere with proper social functioning nor threaten social cohesion) he may not be granted the right to full self-determination in all respects, particularly in matters of life and death. That would fragment society into independent and autonomous units whose existence would atomize society itself.

What could be called the moral value thesis then claims that the survival and welfare of society as a whole take moral precedence over that of any individual member. Since individual sovereignty, in threatening the coherence of the social fabric would thereby threaten society itself, the individual must not have the power of decision in the fundamental matters of life and death. Instead the sovereignty of society must necessarily be absolute in this matter. Euthanasia construed as a decision-option for the individual must therefore be rejected.

Clearly, even this sketch of the argument evinces several flaws. To begin with, the social dynamics thesis may not be correct. There is nothing inherently contradictory about a society consisting of completely sovereign and autonomous individuals who, for survival, mutual aid, gratification, and development interact in more or less regular and regularized ways. Nor must the required ceding of certain rights or privileges by the individual to the group be permanent and absolute; it may be conditional and revocable, for instance, under conditions of agony or in extremis.

Furthermore, it is yet to be proved that society's welfare takes precedence over that of the individual. There is no dearth of contrary hypotheses which assert the complete sovereignty of the individual which present society as at best a necessary evil. These competing hypotheses admit that the individual is integrated into a social fabric but do not require the complete subjugating of the individual's value to that of society. The correctness of the assumption on which the argument from social egoism is based may therefore be questioned; and with it the soundness of the argument as a whole.

SOCIAL DANGER

The preceding considerations focus on a specific socio-dynamic thesis about the continued existence and well-being of society, and deduce that therefore euthanasia must be rejected. There is a similar argument that begins with the psychological attitudes that might be evoked in individual people by the introduction of euthanasia as an instrument of social policy. It maintains that the individual would always perceive a policy of euthanatizing or allowing the moribund, comatose, agonized, mentally severely deviant, or otherwise incurably incapacitated to be euthanatized as a potential threat to his own continued existence. Each person would fear that he might find himself in just that situation—and he would feel instinctive, uncontrollable fears. The policy would inevitably evoke memories of Nazi Germany, people would interpret euthanasia as a way for society to take advantage of those incapable of defending themselves; and ultimately, so it would be feared, the weaker would acquiesce to the dictates of those whom they were physically and psychologically unable to oppose.

However—so the argument continues—there is a commonly accepted opinion, stated by R. Kirk, that "If a social order fails to defend those who cannot defend themselves, then that order is impotent, or heartless, or both" as well, of course, as morally evil. In this argument one sees danger for the social system. If overwhelming fear is indeed the reaction to euthanasia as an instrument of social policy, then social fragmentation will result. The reason is not merely a perceived infringement on personal sovereignty nor the desire for sheer self-preservation but also a perceived breakdown of otherwise sacrosanct social norms. The individual will be confused about a basic belief: While on the one hand society holds up life as the ultimate good and defends it by laws against murder, on the other it disposes of it callously and with apparent disregard. The result is, if not antagonism towards society and social institutions, then at least suspicion and distrust. Even though this may not develop immediately into an overt break with the social structure, the ensuing general unease would seriously undermine the stability of the social fabric; society would gradually granularize into independent individuals acting as laws unto themselves. The ultimate denouement would be the collapse of society as a whole. Since this must be avoided at all cost, euthanasia as a social institution, whether by permission or direction, must be rejected.

Several objections can be raised to this argument. An insistence on facts is the first. While some data do indeed support the contention that people fear a policy of euthanasia, contemporary statistical analyses reveal that the responses of potential euthanasia candidates are not at all that antagonistic or suspicious. Many people favour euthanasia under these circumstances. Rather than seeing it as an exploitation of the weak and helpless, they consider any state that rejects euthanasia or makes it a criminal offence as careless or callously indifferent to the suffering of its citizens. In short, many people—even those who would be subject to its effects—favour the introduction of euthanasia for release from an unbearable, painful, or undignified existence, and so far from resulting in an attitude that would undermine the foundations of social interaction, euthanasia would be seen as an expression of the state's realization of the limits of human endurance and as an acceptance of the duty of care.

Furthermore—so it could be objected—the feelings and attitudes people would allegedly have towards the state if euthanasia were to be legalized are relative rather than absolute. Since the attitude displayed by a given group within society or by society as a whole towards a particular institution or practice is largely a function of conditioning, it can be altered. Attitudes towards life and death are no exception. We need merely consider the fate of suicide legislation and of legislation about abortion to see how this is the case. Therefore euthanasia need not be rejected as a social policy on the grounds that social disorganization would result from the concomitant fear and confusion. Without an appropriate change in conditioning the socially disruptive consequences might well occur—provided, of course, that the theoretical speculations about the social impact of an individual's attitude towards society as a whole are correct. But nothing forces us to keep this conditioning constant. Social conditioning is changed all the time by the various interest groups that dominate society. One could certainly expect that those legislators concerned with legalizing euthanasia would see to it that the relevant emotional reactions and associations were suitably steered. This sort of Orwellian thing is done every day.

However, this last reply is itself open to a general moral objection that applies to the entire argument about social danger. As Jean Dabin puts it "Everybody admits that . . . laws contrary to natural law are bad laws and even that they do not answer to the concept of a law". This argument has it that a law which contradicts the fundamental moral autonomy and integrity of the individual as a moral agent has no proper basis and therefore no compelling moral force, the legal apparatus for its enforcement notwithstanding. Therefore, it is of no moral consequence to argue that enjoining a particular action like euthanasia does or does not affect negatively the survival of a specific society. What has to be shown is that enjoining that act is morally acceptable or unacceptable in the first place. Only then can the question of whether or not a society itself should persist as a result of it be raised. This in turn implies that merely appealing to what people believe, how they react, or how their attitudes affect society is irrelevant in and by itself and that to adduce these as relevant is to beg the question. The question is not whether people will feel threatened and react in certain ways, but whether morally speaking this would be acceptable; it is not whether a certain conditioning can be eradicated and replaced but whether this process and these attitudes are morally correct. It is not that society might collapse but whether the society is worth preserving—and at what price.

The same considerations, mutatis mutandis, apply to a rather famous argument that has enjoyed considerable sociolegal popularity of late. It concentrates on the possible misuse of euthanasia, and is usually called the Wedge.

THE WEDGE

Few arguments against euthanasia are as well known as this one. Sometimes it is called the slippery slope argument, sometimes the slide, but the reasoning is essentially the same: It condemns euthanasia as a whole on the practical social basis that legally permitting a single instance of it would very probably lead to dangerous misuse.

A typical example of the Wedge is found in "The Ethics of Euthanasia":

Once the principle of the sanctity of human life is abandoned, or the propaganda accepted that to uphold it is old-fashioned, prejudicial or superficial, the way is open to the raising of—and the satisfaction of—a demand for so-called euthanasia for the severely crippled, the aged, and ultimately for all who are a burden on community services and the public purse.

Another instance occurs in Yale Kamisar's article "Euthanasia Legislation: Some Non-Religious Objections." Indeed it provides what could almost be considered a classic instance of the argument:

It is true that the "wedge" objection can always be advanced, the horrors can always be paraded. But it is less true that on some occasions the objection is much more valid than it is on others. One reason the parade of horrors cannot be too lightly dismissed in some particular instance is that Miss Voluntary Euthanasia is not likely to be going it alone for very long. Many of her admirers . . . would be neither surprised nor distressed to see her joined by Miss Euthanatize the Congenital Idiot and Miss Euthanatize the Permanently Insane and Miss Euthanatize the Senile Dementia . . . .
Another reason why the "parade of horrors" argument cannot be dismissed in this particular instance . . . is that the parade *has* taken place in our time and the order of procession has been headed by killing the "incurables" and the "useless". . . . The apparent innocuousness of Germany's "small beginnings" is perhaps best shown by the fact that German Jews were at first excluded from the programme. For it was originally conceived that the blessing of euthanasia should be granted only to (true) Germans.

The thrust of this reasoning is that the foot in the door will eventually open it all the way. The slide from acceptable to unacceptable forms of euthanasia is not only conceptually possible but has in fact occurred. We have the example of Nazi horrors before us, and if we wish further indications we need only to look at the potentially dangerous legislation in which the inevitable slide from particular circumscribed permission to general practice has occurred. The use of the various laws dealing with national safety, secrecy and access to information that were in force until quite recently can illustrate the point.

As an emotional appeal to our fears and sensibilities, this argument makes an immediate impact. As a piece of logical reasoning, however, it is unacceptable. To begin with, the present socioeconomic and legal conditions are hardly those of Nazi Germany. At the very least, the totalitarianism and hysteria integral to the German scene of the 1930's are missing. Also, since Germany is not a common-law country what is legally permissible there is not necessarily so here. Therefore the analogy to an allegedly similar situation, from which the argument derives most of its strength, fails. Second, the German motivation was completely different. Whatever justification was given then consisted of racially tinged utilitarianism; now neither racism nor a philosophy of the greatest good for the greatest number of people underlies the pro-euthanasia argument.

But there are also other, purely logical flaws to this sort of reasoning. For instance, the fact that disastrous consequences followed then and there in no way entails that they will also follow in a different situation. The fear of that might be emotionally very real, but without some logical basis of similarity it can never claim to be more than that. Furthermore, as a counter example it could be pointed out that for years capital punishment has merely existed by legal statute, but no such slide has taken place. It is true that just such a perversion of that legal statute has taken place, e.g., in Chile, but the situations are too dissimilar for analogy even to be considered. Therefore one may well ask with some justification, why should such a slide in the case of euthanasia take place here? If the legal killing of persons did not lead to abuse in the one case, why should it lead to misuse in the other?

Finally, there are the following considerations: Any piece of legislation can be misused. What is crucial is how the relevant legislation is interpreted and applied. Given our sociolegal context, perversion of the intent of such legislation would be very difficult. Against it stands the weight of the common-law tradition, which in matters of life and death always has had the interest of the individual as its concern. Finally, the words of David Hume, although intended for a slightly different context, nevertheless are very instructive: "There is no method of reasoning more common, and yet none more blameable, than, in philosophical disputes, to endeavour the refutation of any hypothesis, by a pretence of its dangerous consequences. . . . When any opinion leads to absurdities, it is certainly false; but it is not certain that an opinion is false, because it is of dangerous consequence." This debate then, is really quite beside the point. The issue is not whether it is easy to slide from a limited and responsibly controlled acceptance of euthanasia to political misuse, or whether it is too dangerous a piece of legislation. Instead the question is whether or not euthanasia, however it may be introduced and whatever its socio-legal dangers, is morally right. Assuming a positive answer, the question then becomes who has the right to dispose of the life of the individual. If the individual himself, then society has the corresponding duty to grant him an "easy death" should he so decide; and no misuse of euthanasia on another occasion will detract from either the right or the duty. Even if euthanasia resulted in political misuse or became, in Maguire's words, only a way to "bury the doctors' mistakes," these results by themselves would carry no moral weight; to do so it would have to be proven that they are the inevitable repercussions of the legislated right to euthanasia. And even then, to reject euthanasia on this basis would require still another, still more general moral premise—that the welfare of society as a whole outweighs the rights of the individual.

There is no question that there are theories about the moral interrelationship between man and society that argue just this. Edgar Bodenheimer, for instance, holds that "justice demands that freedom, equality, and other basic rights may be accorded and secured to human beings to the greatest extent consistent with the common good." The *Declaration of Human Rights* states that "In the exercise of his rights and freedoms, everyone should be subject only to such limitations as are determined by law solely for the purpose of securing due recognition and respect for the rights and freedoms of others and of meeting the just requirements of morality [i.e., decency], public order, and the general welfare in a democratic society." But there is also no question that there are opposite moral theories. Those of Kant and Ross provide two outstanding examples, and as John Rawls so clearly put it, "Each person possesses an inviolability founded on justice that even the welfare of society as a whole cannot override. Therefore in a just society the rights secured by justice are not subject to political bargaining or to the calculus of social interests." Unless and until the fundamental differences between these diverse approaches are resolved, the moral status of the socialization of euthanasia as a legal means of terminating life will remain unresolved, and whether the right to this termination will be granted the individual or society as a whole will remain an open question. Therefore until these matters are settled, considerations of social impact are merely raw data awaiting moral evaluation.

LEGISLATION

Closely related to the Wedge is a train of reasoning about the difficulty of legislation. The claim is that euthanasia cannot be made legal without rigid legislative safeguards. The stakes are far too high for the practice to evolve unchecked; the dangers are far too great. However, so the argument continues, it is humanly impossible to write legislation that provides both adequate safeguards and the desired latitude of application. This, at least, is the résumé of several attempts by various organizations in different countries over several decades to achieve such legislation—attempts which failed. The Board of Science and Education of the British Medical Association neatly summarizes their experience: "After careful consideration the panel is convinced that it would be impossible to provide adequate safeguards in any euthanasia legislation"—this from individuals who would ultimately have to implement such legislation. The difficulties of authority alone are overwhelming: Who has the right to decide? The physician? A group of physicians? A hospital committee? The family? The patient? Society as a whole? Some combination of these? None of the alternatives guarantees against religious, social, and even occupational bias. All are so complicated by economic and personal factors that any eventual decision may be unacceptable. Even placing the individual himself as the final authority may not resolve that problem because he may be comatose, insane, or otherwise incommunicado.

A good example of the problems thus envisaged is to be found in the recent California Natural Death Act. Section § 7191 (b) of that act states, "A failure by a physician to effectuate the directive of a qualified patient persuant to this division shall constitute unprofessional conduct if the physician refuses to make the necessary arrangements, or fails to take the necessary steps, to effect the transfer of the qualified patient to another physician who will effectuate the directive of the qualified patient." This clause clearly provides that the wishes of the patient carry the weight of final authority and that a physician who finds himself unable to abide by them is bound to transfer the patient to a physician who will abide by them.

Yet in § 7191 (c) the act goes on to state that,

If the declarant becomes a qualified patient subsequent to executing the directive [for euthanasia], and has not subsequently reexecuted the directive, the attending physician *may* give weight to the directive as evidence of the patient's directions regarding the withholding or withdrawal of life-sustaining procedures *and may consider other factors*, such as information from the affected family or the nature of the patient's illness, or disease, in determining whether the totality of circumstances known to the physician justify effectuating the directive. *No physician, and no licensed health professional acting under the direction of a physician, shall be criminally or civilly liable for failing to effectuate the directive of the qualified patient persuant to this subdivision.*

Thus Section (c), especially its italicized parts, gives the physician discretionary powers which conflict in spirit if not directly with Section (b) above.

This conflict becomes explicit in Section § 7189.5:

A directive shall be effective for five years from the date of execution thereof. . . . If the declarant becomes comatose or is rendered incapable of communicating with the attending physician, the directive shall remain in effect for the duration of the comatose condition or until such time as the declarant's condition renders him or her able to communicate with the attending physician.

This section clearly removes from the attending physician the discretion on whether or not to take the directive at face value. It leaves him only the option, persuant to § 7191 (b), of transferring the individual who "becomes a qualified patient subsequent to executing the directive" to another physician "who will effectuate the directive."

As these considerations demonstrate—so the argument continues—legislating the individual's right to self-determination and at the same time providing for the possibility of error or the patient's change of mind constitute impossible conditions. And yet, none of these conditions can simply be abandoned. The problem of legislation thefore is seen as insurmountable even when some form of consent is present. Matters stand worse for any attempt to legislate euthanasia in cases where informed consent neither was, is, nor can be given—for cases of non-voluntary euthanasia. Since here the dangers of misuse are immeasurably greater, the legislation must be even more stringent. However, common sense alone suggests that if legislation is hopelessly difficult in the case of voluntary euthanasia, it is much more difficult in the case of non-voluntary euthanasia. Therefore—so the argument concludes—it is better to refrain altogether from legislation on euthanasia and simply to trust the accumulation of common-law precedent. That course may be slower—but legally and morally it will be safer.

Another difficulty is, how a physician should judge at what point the patient's request becomes operant. At the present time there is no agreement on this issue; and given the diversity of medical and socio-legal opinion on the concept of life in general, there is likely to be none.

The gist of these objections is clear: It is impossible to have the sufficient, consistent safeguards necessary in a situation of such grave importance without either opening up a Pandora's box of misuse or stultifying the spirit of the legislation. Therefore it is better not to legislate at all than to be faced later with a moral and legal nightmare.

Any attempt to draft euthanasia legislation must recognize these commonly perceived fears as a real impediment to its success. However, objection to such legislation is not confined to opponents of euthanasia. For attempting to provide enabling legislation that is nevertheless within the bounds of safety may well result in too narrow, vacillating, or too uncertain provisions that allow infringement of the legitimate right to death of an individual who is irremediably suffering but not terminally ill. Veatch sees the California act as being thus narrow; it does not allow patients "to have treatment stopped at a time when they are declining and treatment has become burdensome, useless or both, but death is not imminent," and it provides "no assurance that the treatment will be stopped even if one has filled out a document." The comatose individual who has indicated nothing of his will in the matter and the individual who never was legally and morally competent compound the problem. The act does not even consider mercy killing in a non-medical context. An individual may be suffering terminally and horribly on some isolated mountain peak, the victim of a mountaineering accident, far from medical help. Here there is nothing that meets the definitions of "patient," "physician," or "licensed health professional" in the sense of the act, but the need for a decision is just as acute. Is that individual to expire agonizingly because he is not a "patient" or because there is no "licensed health professional"? At the same time is it not possible that doing away with these specific provisions would result in abuse of the act and awful consequences?

Although all these objections are logically correct, those who defend enabling legislation for voluntary euthanasia point out that the dangers envisioned and shortcomings perceived are vastly overestimated in actual fact. For instance, so they argue, Uruguay has had what in effect amounts to such legislation since 1933 and both Germany and Switzerland now have statutes to similar effect. Diligent research would probably turn up more cases, yet in none have the dangers envisioned been realized.

Of course in reply it could always be argued that although such laws exist they are defective, lacking safeguards; that the fact that none of the dangerous consequences has materialized is sheer luck; and that, being dangerous pieces of legislation, they should be repealed. However, several responses are possible: First, it could once again be pointed out that in a common-law tradition like ours the precise import of a given law cannot be assessed until it has been interpreted in the courts; that by its very nature this tradition is a bulwark against a perversion of the rights of the individual; and that therefore any rejection of legislation on these grounds alone is premature.

Second, it could be argued that even if no actual law satisfies all the requirements of internal consistency and coherence it may nevertheless be possible in principle to satisfy them. For there are really only two major sorts of situations that must here be covered: those in which the patient is capable of informed consent and those in which he is not. If the patient is competent, legislation would merely have to recognize his right of self-determination, which, as Charles H. Montange put it, means that "a competent patient . . . [has] the right to redefine his best interests for the duration of a medical procedure," where competence is defined as the patient's ability then and there "to understand the nature, terms, and effect of [his] agreement" or as the "capacity to comprehend his situation, risks, and alternatives." Such legislation would be in agreement with the decision of Mr. Justice Alfred Schroeder of the Kansas Supreme Court, who stated:

Anglo-American law starts with the premise of thoroughgoing self-determination. It follows that each man is considered to be the master of his own body, and he may, if he be of sound mind, expressly prohibit the performance of life-saving surgery, or other medical treatment. A doctor might well believe that an operation or form of treatment is desirable or necessary, but the law does not permit him to substitute his own judgment for that of the patient by any form of artifice or deception.

It would thereby allow a patient to make a decision which seems unreasonable to others. Its provision for the physician's initiating a new course of action at the patient's request in order to procure death would therefore show itself to be nothing more than a logical extension of that same right of "thoroughgoing self-determination." The range of actions thus included would extend to the administration of toxic substances, overdoses of certain drugs or the employment of other techniques to produce death even in situations where death was not imminent. In other words, it would put on the same footing all acts of euthanasia for individuals fulfilling the requirement of competence, and it could be couched in language that would avoid any binding reference to medical personnel or physicians.

In situations where informed consent is not or cannot be given, the law may either assume the decision-making function or appoint a guardian for the individual. That guardian would take into account the latter's expressed wishes (if any) and on advice of a physician (one not connected with the case), a disinterested member of the sociocultural milieu from which the individual comes, and (if possible) a member of the individual's immediate family would then reach a decision as close as possible to what the individual's would have been. Thus either a judge or a legally constituted authority could decide the issue. A "living will," unless expressly countermanded prior to the onset of the problem, should be considered binding in their respective deliberations. Where no will or other indication existed, the decision would have to be reached in accordance with current public norms as understood by the judge or guardian. Legislation currently being drafted in various states indicates that this approach could be implemented. Of course, since such a statute would not fix the particulars of euthanasia for all occasions it could be accused of being vague. However, in that very "vagueness"—or better, in that lack of ultimate specificity—would lie its efficacy and power. If it did attempt to settle the minutiae of all possible circumstances, the very spirit of the law would be blunted by becoming too fixed to a particular context. For, basically, the law must provide a framework that is general enough to cover many different situations. Since the situations change, the law must not be too specific. Otherwise, if it were constructed in any other manner, then by not including it would exclude and therefore would inevitably fail in particular cases. This is not to say that safeguards and limiting provisions should not be built into the statutes. Insofar as it is practicable, they must be. But equally as important as these safeguards are the rights of those who wish for or otherwise are entitled to an easy death. The insistence on safeguards must not be pursued at the cost of ignoring these rights.

Finally, whoever insists on legislative safeguards may be asked to ponder the following questions: May it be that, in claiming that it is impossible to draft a safe enough statute, he is confusing the desire for safeguards with the desire for safety? The desire to punish transgression with the desire to make transgression impossible? No law, however perfect its safeguards, can fulfil the desire for safety. All laws can be broken—not perhaps with impunity, but broken nevertheless. It is impossible in principle to meet the demand for safety by any clause or provision incorporated into the law itself. Therefore to insist on it in the present context would be not merely impractical but also irrational.

More could be said about the difficulty of such legislation: for instance, with respect to the problems of legislating for non-voluntary euthanasia, the spectre of political abuse, the threat of familial and possibly even economic disaster that some see in legalized euthanasia, or the danger of a gradual but inexorable dehumanization of the attitudes of society towards human life. In the main however, these difficulties are not moral but pragmatic and the arguments themselves are vulnerable to the reply that the negative consequences envisioned have not materialized in comparable situations. Furthermore, the issue is not whether such consequences do or will ensue but whether they are morally acceptable. This is not to say that the points raised and issues broached are irrelevant and unimportant. The difficulties that surround the problem of informed consent—to mention but one example—are as important as they are notorious. However they, and indeed the whole problem of decision-making, will remain unresolved until the moral status of euthanasia itself is clarified. To raise them now is to confuse the legal and practical with the moral, to confound what is sociolegally possible with what is right.

UTILITY

There is a series of more theoretical objections to euthanasia that have the principle of utility as their common denominator. This principle maintains that an act is right if and only if it produces or is likely to produce the greatest amount of good for the greatest number of people.

A typical utilitarian argument against euthanasia based on this principle goes something like this: Society as a whole has an interest in preserving the lives of its members from emotional, political, and economic points of view. Thus, the purely emotional harm done to family, friends, and acquaintances—even to the hospital personnel—by introducing euthanasia as a socially acceptable technique would be tremendous. So would the overall impact on society of the awareness that euthanasia was inevitable for the comatose and terminally ill. The resulting outlook would weaken social institutions, and the pecuniary or other advantages allegedly gained by the use of euthanasia would be minimal in comparison. Furthermore, callous as it may sound, the value of a given individual to society is not confined to his own socioeconomic productivity. His presence as an object of research, training, or experimentation may be of tremendous importance. As one physician remarked, not only do we "have to be . . . stringent about keeping people alive in that [terminal] situation because [our] data depends on how long the patient lives," but as Karnofsky put it, we can also "learn a great deal from the study of the patient; . . . [and] even if doctors usually fail, they are kept in training to handle the remediable situations more effectively." In other words the techniques developed in keeping someone alive as long as possible, even against his will, may result in greater good for the whole, even if it is unpleasant for the individual person. Therefore the good that redounds to society from rejecting euthanasia, whether voluntary or otherwise, outweighs the limited good for the affected individual and his immediate associates. The principle of utility, therefore, dictates that the institution of euthanasia must be rejected.

So the argument. However, it is not at all clear that the principle of utility itself necessarily entails such a conclusion. For instance, the resources expended to sustain an individual are by that very token unavailable for other purposes. Therefore considerations of cost as opposed to return, both short- and long-range, must be calculated. Furthermore, social services, productivity, and wealth are all tied up in the research devoted solely to developing better techniques for keeping such individuals alive just a little longer. The resultant techniques in turn, serve only to create a demand for still more and better techniques to keep alive those not as yet benefiting from such research and to extend even further the lives of those who already benefit. However, few if any of those who benefit return anything like a compensatory amount of goods or services to society, nor are the spin-offs of this research of any significant benefit elsewhere. By its very nature it is suited only to extend a little longer the lifespan of those who are terminally ill. Consequently—so this reasoning has it—to reject euthanasia on the basis of the utilitarian considerations adduced in the original argument is illogical. The resources would be committed to something which by its very nature can never have a sum total of positive value and whose side products are inevitably of minimal utilitarian significance. In this light, a general policy of euthanasia, rather than being ruled out, is in fact called for.

Furthermore—so the argument could continue—even if we ignored the involvement in research and the heavy investment in the development of medical knowledge, facilities and expertise, unbiased utilitarian calculations in general favour euthanasia. Medical budgets are not limitless; neither are family budgets nor those of the society which has to pay for the hospitals and services. How much will medical intervention cost? What is the likelihood of success? What is the projected rate of social return? The three horsemen of the medical apocalypse. As Eliot Slater wrote about euthanasia for children with *spina bifida*: "The death . . . costs nothing; the life costs not only money but the preemption of precious medical, nursing, social and educational resources." The same point applies to a majority of other cases.

Of course it is not usually stated quite so bluntly. Instead we are invited to consider the fact that the "extraordinary" means necessary for keeping such an individual alive are "very costly, or very painful, or very difficult, or very dangerous;" or we are exhorted to adopt a position of robust ethical common sense since after all, as Joseph Fletcher put it, ethics "cannot escape calculative interests, playing the numbers game, nose or head counting," In other words, we are told that there is a point of diminishing returns beyond which it is unreasonable for the family and society in general to go in the investment of capital; a point beyond which no individual may lay claim to an expenditure of resources. Such cases include the thalidomide babies and persons suffering from Huntington's chorea or multiple sclerosis, individuals severely brain-damaged by drug overdoses, effectively decerebrated accident victims, those suffering from senile dementia, those who because of some brain dysfunction have slipped into an irremediable coma, or those who are dying of incurable and advanced cancer. The resources these demand far outstrip what in the end are absolutely minimal returns. The problem is not merely whether a particular family can afford to pay for the care of a specific individual, for even the richest of families actually contribute only a fraction of the total economic expense. The necessary research, the medical experts, and the general medical facilities are communal resources. Therefore the underlying issue really is whether—and to what degree— an individual has a right to the resources of society as a whole.

The nature of the good which tacitly forms the core of the utilitarian reasoning also constitutes a point of difficulty for the various arguments. Physical well-being is by no means the only good. As John Stuart Mill pointed out, "Human beings have faculties more elevated than the animal appetites" of food, sex, and comfortable physiological surroundings. As "beings of higher faculties," they require more than merely these to make them happy. But however this "more" is ultimately spelled out, in the end "its most appropriate appellation is a sense of dignity, which all human beings possess in one form or another." That sense of dignity involves the rational human nature, and any state of affairs that offends it amounts to its denial which amounts to disutility. Therefore any action that detracts from the full realization of this aspect of human nature has an amount of disutility proportional to the degree and extent of its interference with that realization. Now, all of us die. In some cases the advent of death is premature and preventable. When this is not the case however, the attempt to sustain the individual may be possible only by just such an affront to his "sense of dignity." Situations involving the hopelessly agonized, terminally ill, and irrevocably comatose are good examples. In these cases euthanasia would not only do away with physical pain and suffering—which in itself is of positive utility—but would also accord that sense of dignity. Therefore when these non-socioeconomic and non-physiological considerations enter into the calculations of utility, euthanasia frequently emerges as a socially acceptable practice. To conclude otherwise here would be to ignore this qualitative component of utility.

At this point utility merges with the possible social danger of a policy of euthanasia. For if fear of social disruption is subject to conditioning, so is the perception of euthanasia as deleterious to research, medical advances, and the emotional stability of family, friends, and hospital staff. Attitudes then should be changed so the average citizen sets dignity

above length of life and views the continued attempt to sustain the comatose as what it is: an unrealistic and undignified manipulation of a human
being who is better off dead. There is little utility in denying death.

Once again, however, the reasoning is vulnerable. How much of its
appeal to common sense and reasonableness resides in the situation itself,
and how much is emotional appeal? Would those who propose that
utilitarianism requires euthanasia on purely economic grounds use this
economic criterion as a generic social principle? Would they be willing to
accept it in all those cases in which there is an inadequate return for the
investment, when it is too expensive or burdensome to keep an individual
alive? The general maxim would demand this. It is very doubtful, however,
that many of its proponents would continue to defend it, thus boldly
stated. In our society, at least, there is considerable reluctance about
such a blatant cost-profit approach to death.

Furthermore, the counterargument may be attacked. For example,
it is insufficiently precise to claim that keeping the terminal patient alive
wastes socioeconomic resources without adequate return; or to claim that
the individual whose life is at stake or the physician or society may decide
that the economic burden is too great. Any claim of proportion is relative
to a given purpose. Since the primary purpose of society, so it could be
argued, is to ensure the survival of its members for as long as possible,
the utility of investing socioeconomic resources in this direction must
be weighted proportionally higher than an expenditure of these same
resources in any other way. Rather than being disproportionate, therefore,
the investment becomes precisely proportionate because it is directed
towards the fulfilment of society's primary aim. And that, so this argument could continue, can hardly be touted as a disutilitarian state of
affairs.

The rejoinder that survival as the primary aim of society refers not to
the survival of its individual members but to the corporate entity, the
society as a whole, is itself vulnerable to the reply that society, unlike
culture, is the totality of people in relation *here and now*. It is not distinct
from its members. It consists not only of the well, the able, and the
productive but also of the ill, the very young and the very old, the debilitated, comatose, and terminally ill—in short, of *all* the people that
are socially interrelated. Its existence, nature, and character are determined by the natures and extant relations of its members. As individuals
come into being and pass away, as the relations among the members
change, so does society itself. Therefore society must necessarily try to
ensure its members' existence for the sake of its own. Since that existence
is a function of the existence of these very members, it must deploy its
resources towards their survival. Consequently, so this argument continues,

it is precisely the debilitated and ill citizens who should receive society's sustaining efforts. They are the ones who need it. To argue differently would be either to relegate the primary aim of society—preservation—to a position of inferior importance (or deny it altogether) or to confuse *society*—namely, the people in social context—with *culture*: the qualitative nature of the interrelations themselves. Only the latter can survive without a specific group of individuals just as long as there are individuals at all; the former is dependent on the identity of the individuals themselves. Therefore its primary purpose makes society's expenditure of resources in support of those who require it neither disproportionate nor misplaced. There simply could not be a logically more appropriate investment.

Furthermore—so this line of reasoning might continue—more than mere survival enters into assessing the correct expenditure of society's resources. Simply to function, society requires a web of right-duty relationships between it and its members and among the members themselves. These relationships are reciprocal. The individual has duties towards society, and society has corresponding obligations towards the individual. Not the least important of these is the obligation to ensure the individual's life and welfare. Since this obligation derives from a reciprocal relationship, it cannot be abrogated unilaterally but only mutually. Euthanasia for utilitarian reasons, therefore, cannot be a legitimate exercise of society's duties towards the individual. Instead these interrelations mean that it will be society's duty to preserve the individual's life even if that should be difficult or inconvenient for the others. After all, *that* such an effort be made when it becomes necessary is part of the condition of accepting membership in the society in the first place, and no unilateral claim of disutility or inconvenience will later do away with this obligation.

QUALITY OF LIFE

The argument about the quality of social life as affected by euthanasia usually involves considerations of the deleterious effect on the quality of social life in general when euthanasia is not used as well as considerations of the inequitable availability of medical resources to the various groups when euthanasia is not practical. Not using euthanasia means concentrating disproportionately society's finite resources on terminally ill people, with a corresponding economic deprivation in other areas of social concern, and following inevitably, a drop in the qualitative standards that are possible in those other domains. What is more, the current tendency is to channel more and more resources into the care of what would otherwise be considered moribund patients. The lifestyle of society as a whole, therefore, if not affected now, will sooner or later suffer in both a qualitative and a quantitative sense. In fact, this is already happening in some places. Therefore it is prudent and morally right to stop sustaining the comatose and terminally ill at the cost of others' life quality and to euthanatize them in some appropriate way.

The same conclusion comes from a consideration of the inequitable availability of medical resources. In our society the access that people from lower socioeconomic strata have to adequate medical services is uneven, to say the least. Not all people benefit from society's involvement in the medical sphere. Only the economically privileged, who can afford insurance premiums, or physicians, and hospital bills, are adequately served. M. C. Weinstein and W. B. Stason nicely describe the situation:

Consumers argue that health is a right, and physicians argue that their duties are to provide everything for their patients regardless of cost. These arguments are tenable for the patients who are fully covered by insurance and fee-for-service physicians because they receive medical care free. For those in society who must bear the ever-increasing cost of health care, however, these arguments do not hold.

They also do not hold because, whatever the premiums or fees, ultimately the major part of medical services is supported and paid by the underprivileged and lower socioeconomic classes. Through direct taxation and the indirect means of economic intercourse, they not only make funds available to governmental agencies and the granting bodies which support medical research, construction, and education, but they also enable the more privileged members of society to attain their favoured socioeconomic niche. Herein lies the injustice: By those very economic facts which make all of this possible, the underprivileged individuals find themselves deprived of the funds to pay for the insurance and other premiums that are placed on the medical services made possible by their direct and indirect contributions. Those facilities and services therefore are open not to those who are ultimately responsible for them but only to the privileged few. This of course is objectionable. Even more objectionable however, is the exclusive allocation of many medical funds for research, services, and facilities to care for and keep alive the terminal and moribund. This drains resources away from medical undertakings that could in principle provide some benefit to the lower socioeconomic classes, perhaps by a filtering down of certain techniques. It reserves resources for projects that could not conceivably have a universally beneficial effect.

There are, of course, several ways to correct this situation. The most obvious and most equitable would be to restructure the whole system of medical services, techniques, and delivery so that everyone has truly equal access. That, however, is a momentous undertaking which would probably require a radical reorganization of the whole social fabric. Failing that, we can stop spending our resources on saving the incurably ill. We can euthanatize. Consequently euthanasia in all the sorts of cases mentioned should be standard practice on all social levels: Once a certain point of permanent physiological or mental debility has been reached, the individual should be allowed to die if already terminal and otherwise should be pleasantly put to death. Only in that way can a proper quality of life be guaranteed all citizens and an equitable distribution of medical services be guaranteed.

So the argument. However, both quality of life and equitable distribution of medical services as bases for euthanasia present the same basic ethical problem: the acceptability of utilitarianism. Does providing high-quality life for a majority of people take precedence over the lives of a given few? Yes, if utility is the guideline. If the larger group's quality of life would be appreciably improved if the smaller were either directly done to death or simply allowed to die, then that course of action is not only morally preferable but mandatory.

The cynic would reply that the principle demands homicide for the sake of social convenience. But unless such action is taken, will not the underprivileged remain qualitatively deprived in their lifestyle and the disadvantaged deprived of services that are rightly theirs? After all, continued deprivation will result in worse socioeconomic conditions leading to worse health, leading to worse ability, leading to worse conditions, ad infinitum. Is it not true that "social interests are best served by using [the] limited health care resources in the most efficacious way possible?" Do not "health services of marginal value only have to be denied" to achieve a more reasonable, effective, and equitable distribution? Does not the medical care of potential euthanasia candidates consume disproportionately large amounts of medical services and thereby drain away these resources from the underprivileged sectors who cannot afford proper day-to-day medical and infant care? And does this not result in a lifestyle that perpetuates bad health and a shortened life span?

The fact of such a drain cannot be denied. Any allocation of social resources is at the expense of some sector of social endeavour, and medical resources are no exception. Nor can it be denied that there are more cost-effective ways for society to expend its resources than to sustain the sorts of individuals mentioned. Furthermore, the cost of research and development of techniques is indeed borne by the broad middle and lower socioeconomic base of society, just as is the training of the physicians and technicians who ultimately employ them. Finally, the philanthropic munificence that builds hospital wings, endows research, and supports medical projects is possible only because of our socioeconomic structure: The capital is gained by economic intercourse with the less privileged classes, and these projects themselves redound to further economic benefit to the more privileged few. Therefore it is true that ultimately this broad class pays.

However, instead of showing that therefore euthanasia should become an instrument of social policy, all this establishes precisely that conclusion which was rejected as unrealistic above: that the resource distribution of our society in general, and particularly that of its medical services, is faulty, that therefore it should be altered in such a way that no one is treated unfairly and the exploitation of the lower socioeconomic classes for the sake of the higher is not continued. While all of this would of course require restructuring not only our current medical delivery system but also delivery of resources in general, it does not require utopian discoveries and upheavals. We only need overcome social inertia and traditional preconceptions. Finally, even if socioeconomic upheavals were required, would not the fact that anything else would be an unjust course of action demand that we undertake them?

This reply, however, assumes that society in fact has sufficient resources both to care for the irrevocably comatose and terminally ill on the one hand and at the same time to secure an equitable lifestyle of acceptable quality for all. In an ideal and adequately supplied society this would be possible, but what of societies where, no matter how much resources are shifted and redirected and the fabric of socioeconomic intercourse adjusted, the resources are simply inadequate to fulfil all purposes? Many contemporary societies find themselves in this situation. Therefore the same old questions arise once again: Does the quality of life of the many not take precedence over the life of the few? Particularly if membership in the latter group is the result of social inequity in any case? The question is the same even when only limited resources are involved and not inequity.

The issue therefore reveals itself for what it really is: a triage conflict. That is why many hold with Weinstein and Stason that we have no choice but to mention "human lives and dollars in the same breath and [to set] cost-effectiveness criteria." For realistic and responsible decisions must be made not haphazardly but on the basis of criteria. What more relevant criteria are there in this context than the capacity of an individual, if kept alive, to participate meaningfully in social intercourse, to become a productive member of society? Nor can we simply ignore the social ramifications of the quality of his mental and physical life were he to be saved or sustained. Furthermore, must we not balance all this against the probable benefits of a different distribution of the resources—an equation which would include the projected length of the individual's survival and the temporal span of the expected results in the alternative case. Nose and head counting, it may thus be argued, are really the only criteria that make any sense under the circumstances. Some who oppose this utilitarianism, convinced of the absolute value of human life, may here see biology as encroaching on the humanistic sphere and would argue with Albert Schweitzer that "the ethics of the social sciences, which is no longer based on an ethics of the individual, can only determine that the progress of society goes according to relentless laws at the cost of the freedom and happiness of the individual. It is the doctrine of being sacrificed." They would concur in his ultimate conclusion that "ethics goes only as far as humanity, which is to say respect for the existence and happiness of the individual human being. Where humanity stops, a pseudo-ethics sets in." Others, however, equally as opposed to the utilitarian position, may reject the cost-effectiveness approach not because of any absolute value of human life—whatever that may mean—but because the problem really lies in the domain of obligations and rights.

Still other replies are, of course, possible. As many as there are diverse ethical positions. The preceding does, however, indicate the arena in which the final decision must be made. Which moral stance is correct? But having said this, I shall leave the matter for the time being, to return to it in more detail later.

THE MALTHUSIAN ARGUMENT

The problem of overpopulation, which Malthus foresaw, has received support from recent predictions by the Club of Rome. The threat of overpopulation is only too real. There is an argument for euthanasia that is based on this. It is expressed by R. H. Williams as follows: "Our goal should not be to prolong every life as long as possible . . . We must consider whether such prolongation leads to happiness or to great physical or mental suffering for the patient and others. We must also consider social, economic and other concerns of society, *including the imminent problem of overpopulation*." [author's emphasis]

Here as in the preceding arguments, the fact of resource limitation plays a fundamental role. The argument itself, then, can be put like this: The resources of every society whether global or parochial, industrialized or fellahin—indeed, the resources of the world—are limited. Therefore unlimited growth is impossible. It will be bought at the price of famine, then pestilence, and finally death. Of course there are various ways to control population growth. Birth control is the most obvious, although not the only one accepted. However, for sociodynamic reasons the growth rate of a society cannot be kept to zero. Like an organism, a society that does not produce new members dies. But there is this group of people whose very existence constitutes a disproportionate burden on the resources of society. What is more, this burden is imposed without ultimate benefit to society as a whole. If the comatose, severely mongoloid, and terminally ill were deleted, the finite resources of society would last and the threat of overpopulation disappear. Consequently, since these "have lived" and in any case are unnecessary, they should be euthanatized. As Maguire puts it in a rhetorical question, "Could a moral obligation then arise to terminate one's life responsibly?"

The factual premises here are unexceptionable. The world's resources are finite, they are beginning to run out. A significantly large amount of these resources—resources which would keep alive whole populations dying of starvation—is indeed devoted to saving terminal individuals. Nevertheless, parts of this argument are unacceptable. For instance, euthanasia as a method of population control could not be a substitute for effective birth control. Even if euthanasia were made mandatory for everyone at a certain age or state of debilitation, an unchecked birth-rate would be higher than the corresponding voluntary and obligatory death rate. Furthermore, to compare society to a living organism is illegitimate. Societies are not trees: the metaphor is only a metaphor. And although most social growth is indeed numerical, in Scandinavia, for instance, where population has been relatively constant without the practice of euthanasia, growth is seen as a function of socialization. Furthermore, that euthanasia as a Malthusian measure would be morally acceptable, assuming it did work, remains unproven. Finally, euthanatizing the useless and debilitated in the interest of potential healthy beings requires that we treat the unborn potential beings as though they were actual and as though some harm would be done if their existence were prevented. This is nonsense. Entities that do not exist as persons cannot have any rights; not even the right to existence. If they did, anybody interfering with that right would incur moral guilt. In that case all of us would be guilty since by refraining from procreating at every possible moment we would be depriving an individual of his right to life. As to the argument that we have the duty toward generations as yet unborn to make the quality of their lives as pleasant as possible—a claim sufficiently familiar from current conservationists' debates—this too is not telling. Because these generations do not yet exist, they cannot have what duties must rest on, which is an existence or a certain nature. Therefore we do not have duties towards them. What we do have is a conditional duty:

If we do bring new individuals into the world, *then* it is our duty to do our best by them once they exist. However, since we have no absolute duty to bring anyone into existence—the Biblical injunctions to be fruitful and multiply being religious, not moral—we do not have the duty to kill anyone in order to bring these potential beings into existence or to provide for them a certain quality of life.

The Malthusian argument therefore fails to establish that euthanasia is obligatory to control population. Obviously, matters might stand differently if there were some absolute duty to increase society, but no such duty exists.

EUGENICS

Although contemporary medicine can control or eradicate many diseases like smallpox, and amniocentesis can detect many genetic maladies prior to birth, as yet not all diseases can be dealt with in this way and some of them manifest themselves only years later in life. These facts underlie the argument from eugenics, summarized by Yale Kamisar:

The welfare of society takes precedence over the welfare and even existence of its individual members. The breeding back into the common gene pool of deleterious genes such as those of Huntington's chorea, Tay-Sachs disease and the like ultimately jeopardizes the welfare of society as a whole, both in a qualitative sense as well as from the point of view of survival. Therefore these and similar genes ought to be deleted permanently from the gene pool. Consequently unpleasant as it may be, the individuals carrying these genes ought to be killed.

Like all other arguments discussed so far, this one is based on fact: So far as we know, certain genes are deleterious to the welfare and survival of society. However, in spite of this, the proffered conclusion does not follow. First, the argument presents as *the* solution what in fact is only one of several alternatives—and some would say the worst possible alternative. Strictly enforced breeding laws and compulsory sterilization of all who evince the undesirable genetic characteristics are just as possible and would achieve a similar effect at much smaller cost. Why then euthanasia? Abortion would be the logical alternative. However, the genetic disabilities in question manifest themselves some time after birth. We would therefore be dealing with young people and adults. But then, surely the remedy proposed would not be effective. These people would already have reached maturity, particularly in cases like Huntington's chorea, and by the time their genetic debility were discovered in all probability they would have had children. To opt for euthanasia here would be like locking the barn after the horses have gone. Only a rigorously controlled breeding programme would work. But it too has dangers. Genes crosslink. Therefore until we are quite certain that no survival characteristics are crosslinked with the allegedly deleterious ones we had best refrain from exclusive breeding practices, let alone euthanasia.

In this connection it should also be noted that what superficially appears to be a deleterious or even lethal gene in one context constitutes a survival factor in another, as sickle-cell anemia has shown. Furthermore, all of us carry recessive genes about which we know very little but which may well be deleterious. A programme of eugenics would require that every one of us who has a genetically deviant ancestor should be killed. Since after approximately two hundred generations most of us share the same ancestors, it follows that most of us would belong to this group.

Finally the unwelcome consequences of this argument can also be brought out in the following way. For every natural disease there is a group of individuals who have a natural immunity to it. Susceptibility to a given disease therefore indicates an absence of such immunity. Most people are susceptible to some debilitating or fatal disease like bubonic plague, poliomyelitis, or typhoid. Parity of reasoning would therefore demand that all those not naturally immune to these so-called killer diseases be themselves killed since, lacking the gene for immunity, they would be judged genetically faulty. It is highly doubtful that society would survive the resultant mass euthanasia. The religious objections to such a programme are obvious. The absurdity of the conclusion speaks for itself.

FAMILY IMPACT

Because in our society the relationship of the family to its individual members is assumed to be very special in a biological as well as a moral sense, the wishes and opinions of family members are generally thought to be relevant in a privileged way when it comes to deciding the fate of the comatose or moribund patient.

These assumptions form the basis of the argument that the comatose or moribund be euthanatized out of consideration for the rest of the family. The argument goes like this: The burden of sustaining a permanently comatose individual, of caring for and attempting to keep alive a terminally ill family member, or of supporting someone who requires continued hemodialysis, the use of a respirator, and the like is staggering. Even though society assumes the greater financial burden, enough remains to make the financial position of all but the wealthiest of families precarious. The necessary sacrifices of material goods, career, and comfort are great; and added to these are psychological stresses. Conflict, depression, and resentment produce a strain that is well-nigh unbearable, affecting both mental and physical health. Therefore fairness and consideration for the quality of life of the other family members require that the individuals who give rise to this be allowed or given a peaceful and pleasant end.

Obviously, this reasoning is open to criticism. From the religious quarter comes the rejoinder that not all values are material and that not all goods are self-directed. The parable of the Good Samaritan, we are told, makes it quite clear that we owe our neighbour a duty of care. Furthermore —so we are exhorted—placing the good of the other family members ahead of that of the suffering comatose member may mean ignoring an opportunity for moral and spiritual growth. Also, to intervene actively or passively in terminating someone's life would be to interfere with the intended course of nature: with God's design. It might even be argued that the claim that such a patient would be better off dead presupposes full knowledge of the moral structure of reality independently of revelation, since revelation expressly forbids killing. That, so the argument continues, smacks of heresy.

The philosophical or moral response to this sort of reasoning is that to treat human life as part of a formula that includes money, careers, and happiness means treating people as things. Furthermore, the duties of family members cannot simply be ignored at the whim or pleasure of one of the parties if it is to his advantage. In fact, it is in precisely this sort of context that the individual's rights enter into full force and require from the family a fulfilment of its obligation.

The social retort is that to disrupt the family, the basic unit of our society, is to disrupt society itself and ultimately to cause its dissolution. Euthanasia, however, would dissolve the family's supportive, caring role and strike at its very core. Therefore society would be jeopardized. However as Thomas Hobbes so aptly put it, life outside society would be "solitary, nasty, brutish and short." Consequently, if only for the reason of sheer survival euthanasia ought to be rejected.

Finally, from a purely logical point of view, the argument falls into the trap of presenting euthanasia as the only way to solve the conflict between the good of the patient and the good of the family. However, that conflict may be resolved in another way. If a person is a unit of society; if in bringing this individual into existence not only the family but also the society incurred an obligation; then it may be claimed that when (as here) the need arises, society must fulfil its obligations: It must not permit the family to be torn asunder by a misfortune not of its devising, and it must look after the individual's welfare. The family acquired its commitments as agents of the society when bringing the individual into existence in the first place. Consequently society will have to assume the burden of support if the family would otherwise suffer financially, psychologically, or personally. At the same time it must also ensure the individual's welfare. Of course implementation of this sort of solution would involve the restructuring and even re-evaluation of the interrelationship between society, family, and the individual. That, however, may not be a bad thing, particularly if the alternative is murder for the sake of convenience.

SOCIETY'S GREATER GOOD

The initial issue remains unresolved: Is there a limit to what society must spend? If so what is it, and why? And if not, why not? In an article entitled "Technological Devices in Medical Care," Fletcher made the following assertion "Ethical plain speaking calls for a hardnosed formula: the welfare of the many comes before the welfare of the few; if you prefer, the individual may rightly be sacrificed to the social good. It is ethical infantilism to suppose that there is a comfortable harmony between the private and the social interest." Fletcher then suggested that euthanasia is called for in many instances of terminal or comatose patient care. Williams argrees with him: "Our goal should not be to prolong every life as long as possible . . . We must consider whether such prolongation leads to happiness or to great mental suffering for the patient and others. We must also consider social, economic and other concerns of society, including the imminent problem of overpopulation." The underlying point of view is clear: If the general good of society requires it, then the terminal, comatose, or otherwise seriously debilitated patient should be allowed to die or be killed.

These are actually considerations of utility: the greatest good for the greatest number. The danger of utilitarian convictions, particularly in the context of life and death, is that what actually is an overrriding concern for the welfare of mankind may look like logical and socioeconomic callousness; that the fact that the sacrifice of the individual may be required for the greater good of the whole may be interpreted as indifference towards the welfare of the individual. However, the contrary is true. Precisely because there is concern for the individual is the good of the totality deemed greater than that of any one particular person. For—so the reasoning seems to be—not to value the good of the greater higher than that of the lesser number would be to denigrate the value of the individuals themselves.

Hopefully, these remarks will clarify one of the most important motivations underlying acceptance of the utilitarian stance in medical ethics. But while it may clarify, it does not make the theory itself immune from criticism. As Fletcher points out, any utilitarian position "cannot escape calculative interests, playing the numbers game, nose or head counting." It must place numerical value on people in order to calculate the private and public goods. However, opposition crystallizes at just this point: the incummensurable value of rational beings.

Furthermore, there are various types of utilitarianism. All of them share the basic premise that an act is right if and only if it promotes the greatest good for the greatest number of people. They differ in how they define and evaluate this good. Rule utilitarianism applies general rules to society as a whole and thus guarantees consistency. Act utilitarianism, on the other hand, insists on the uniqueness of every situation and argues that calculations of utility are necessary for each and every act on each and every occasion. Hedonistic utilitarianism claims that the good aimed at by utilitarianism is simply pleasure, which would increase if the comatose and terminal patients were killed off, freeing the resources they drain from society. Ideal utilitarianism holds that the traditional Judaeo-Christian virtues are goods higher than the material; in this light, euthanasia might well be counterutilitarian and should be rejected. Therefore, even if utilitarianism as a general theory is correct, which particular type of utilitarianism is supposed to be followed? Unless and until this issue is settled any argument based on utilitarianism as a general theory is open to question.

Another problem is this: The argument claims that not to engage in euthanasia in certain cases amounts to choosing disutility over utility and therefore is morally reprehensible. In support of this claim, which is crucial to the argument, economy and a general drain on resources are cited as decisive factors. However, not only must utility be demonstrated in the immediate context in which euthanasia is contemplated, but it must also be shown that the whole social fabric involved will suffer before any claim to disutility can be accepted. Furthermore, even if a method to calculate human good existed, it might not favour euthanasia. The assertion that it would, as the argument suggests, can be proved only by actual calculations. Until these are in, the matter has far too serious consequences to be decided on the basis of a mere claim. After all, no matter how utility is construed, there is more to the good than is encompassed in the immediately available material resources: Future considerations are also relevant. Consequently, we must wait and see.

A much more general but still important question is whether society as a whole should have a certain level of amenities, a certain high quality. That is to say, according to utilitarianism, social interest comes before private interest and the individual's welfare and survival must not be bought at the price of the welfare of society as a whole. However, so the argument maintains, any redistribution and rechanneling of resources to save someone who would otherwise be a candidate for death interferes deleteriously with the welfare of society. Therefore, in the face of these threats no such redistribution should take place.

This reasoning assumes that a particular qualitative level of social amenities is a good thing and that whatever disturbs it is unjust. But what guarantees the correctness of this contention? Is this a basic socio-moral contention which in and by itself is intuitively obvious? Obviousness is a function of conditioning and individual preference—matters of psychological interest at best. They have no moral import. If reasoning—perhaps one which reduces to the thesis about the absolute status of human life—is involved, the enquiry is merely pushed back one step further, and we can demand a reasoned defence of this thesis. Even somehow linking this reasoning to the survival of society itself—perhaps by arguing that a certain minimal qualitative standard is necessary and that without it society will collapse in a series of self-seeking and self-preserving acts—will not be sufficient. It must first be shown that society—not the individual members but society itself—is worth preserving. If this is not done, the whole reasoning will be without basis.

What can we conclude from all this? First, purely logically speaking, none of these arguments, whether for or against euthanasia is particularly convincing. In most cases the step from premise to conclusion is taken too hastily or requires additional premises of dubious moral acceptability. Second, the various arguments frequently disagree on their facts. Even when they agree they differ on what the facts entail. Third, the overall moral framework of the particular arguments is never clearly presented, let alone examined. The ultimate solution to the problem of euthanasia, however, even as raised from a social point of view—if indeed such a solution is possible—requires a close look at the various ethical frameworks, both in their theoretical aspects as well as with respect to their social ramifications.

4

PERSONHOOD

In argumentation dealing with euthanasia, whether this be for or against, the claim that an individual is or is not a person is frequently taken to have considerable bearing on the moral facts at issue: Not merely with respect to the determination of general policy but also as a factor of immediate practical significance, affecting the moral evaluation of a specific case. For instance, according to one argument personhood carries with it a special moral status that rules out the very possibility of euthanasia, whether voluntary or non-voluntary: Persons are ends in themselves, and to euthanatize them would be to deny their status as persons, making them means to an end. Another line of reasoning contends that precisely because persons enjoy this moral status we ought to opt for euthanasia in certain contexts; a person is a unique moral entity to whom we owe a fair and easy death in the appropriate instances. Alternately, it is argued that persons are indeed ends in themselves but that the body is a purely biological entity and may be euthanatized. Since in many instances we are faced with only a body, the refusal to euthanatize results from confusing personhood with humanity, from failing to see that the individual in question—for instance, a severely and irreparably brain-damaged individual —is merely a biological organism and no longer a person. The rejoinder to this is that the distinction between human biological organism and person is itself mistaken because it rests on limited understanding. The fact is that personhood and biological humanity are inseparable. So long as there is human life there is personhood; and since the life of a person has absolute value, human life has absolute value as well. Therefore under no circumstances is it allowable to kill or to let die, since that amounts to the same thing.

Even if we agree with one of these conclusions, it would be acceptable only theoretically. The facts stand differently. Often we must simply decide who is to live and who is to die. The situations themselves allow no choice. And here we simply must have criteria for selection. The most manageable criterion is the human being/person distinction. Therefore, since we have no other pragmatically useful choice, we must accept as a live option the principle of euthanasia as based on lack of personhood.

ENDS AND MEANS

There are two sorts of positions which hold that a person is an end in himself and may therefore never be euthanatized. One maintains that persons are ends in themselves because all living beings are: Since all life is sacred, human beings must not be killed. The other holds that only the lives of human beings have special value because only human beings are persons, or ends in themselves. Albert Schweitzer defended the first of these because he claimed that all life is sacred: "The ethics of respect for life does not recognize any relative ethics. It admits as good only the preservation and advancement of life. All destruction and harming of life, no matter what the circumstances under which this may occur, it designates as evil." This argument of course entails that all of us will inevitably become morally guilty since we must kill—even if only plants and microbes—in order to stay alive: i.e., in order to avoid the guilt of our death. Schweitzer himself appears to have been aware of this consequence because he continued, "[This ethics] does not absolve man of conflicts but forces him to decide in each case for himself how far he may remain moral and how far he must subjugate himself to the necessity of the destruction and the harming of life." However, we may legitimately wonder how such a claim of the necessity of moral guilt could ever be established in view of the fact that some sort of act, be it overt or covert, direct or indirect, is inevitable in any situation. Even not to act is to affect events and therefore act. An ethical theory, however, that thus predetermines moral guilt results from an insufficiently close analysis of the nature of moral acts. Alternately, the argument leading up to it may itself be considered a reductio ad absurdum of the inviolability of all life.

The allegedly unique moral status of a person's life is put forward most powerfully and consistently by Immanuel Kant. He was concerned with suicide, but the parallel with euthanasia is clear:

If, in order to escape from burdensome circumstances, we were to kill someone or he asked to be destroyed, we/he should be using a person merely as a means to maintaining a tolerable condition to the end of life.

Man, however, is not a thing, and therefore not something that may be used merely as a means, but in all acts must forever be considered an end in itself. Therefore we/he cannot dispose of a human being in our/his person so as to mutilate, corrupt or kill him.

According to this sort of position, then, there is something contradictory about the claim that we are killing an individual for his own sake. For, to do something for someone for his own sake is to consider him an end in himself; whereas to kill him is always to end his life for a further reason or purpose, namely the tolerable condition mentioned by Kant. Therefore, if using a person as a means to an end is morally reprehensible, then euthanasia will be so as well.

That, however, is a very large if indeed. It is not at all clear why the fact that something is an end in itself should have any moral significance. Nor does Kant's own explanation help:

An end [in itself] must . . . be conceived not as an end to be produced, *but as a self-existent end.* It must therefore be conceived only negatively — that is, as an end against which we should never act . . . and consequently as one which in all our willing we must never rate *merely* as a means, but always at the same time as an end.

An end in itself here seems to be a being that has absolute or intrinsic worth. But this merely prompts us to reiterate the question: Why should whoever possesses this intrinsic worth therefore have a special moral status? If someone has intrinsic worth, it may be inappropriate, unwise, or foolhardy to make of him a means to an end, but that is not necessarily a moral matter. For a moral consequence to follow, what is required is a properly moral premise: Perhaps something like, it is morally reprehensible to treat entities that have intrinsic value as though they did not. This premise, however, is no more plausible than the initial claim. One could still argue with perfect reasonableness that such a premise was simply wrong; that this sort of treatment of an end in itself would not be morally objectionable but simply misguided or inappropriate. One might even attempt to diagnose this moral reasoning as faulty because it rests on a confusion over wherein the basis of moral relationship lies. That it lies not in the notions of good and value, but in the notion of right.

However, even if we accepted the moral link between having intrinsic worth and being an end in oneself, we could not conclude that euthanasia is therefore proscribed. For there are neither ends in themselves nor absolute values. All values are relative, as are all ends. They are artificial human constructs: something that we project onto a morally and value theoretically completely neutral world.

But suppose that we were willing to admit that a person has intrinsic worth and therefore should not be used as a means to an end, or euthanatized. Still the argument would fail. For how precisely could we be said to be using a person as a means to an end when we act as purveyors of euthanasia? Even granted the meaningfulness of that notion, it could still be argued that to kill a person in order to end what is for him an unbearable state of affairs is not to use *him* as a means to an end. It is merely to end a particular state of affairs—his suffering—for a particular reason: in order to spare him further suffering, indignity, and the like. This is so whether he is thought to be a soul, a complex of body and soul, or merely a body. Thus neither he nor his death is a means. His future state—his non-existence—could perhaps be construed as a means to sur-cease from indignity, suffering, or pain. That, however, would be stretching language to the breaking point. The concept of means makes sense only with respect to tools or devices, such as poison, a knife, even the withdrawing of treatment or medication.

Furthermore, the argument becomes absurd when its point is gen-eralized: the same reasoning would entail that whenever someone relieves pain by administering an analgesic, relieves hunger by giving food, or removes any physiological malfunction by the appropriate medical tech-nique he too is using an individual as the means to an end. After all, the latter state is radically affected by an alteration of the individual himself. But, clearly, to call someone immoral because he alleviated the hunger pangs of the starving or reduced someone's pain, is ridiculous. In which case, so is claiming that a person who engages in euthanasia to end some-one's agony. The charge of using him as a means to an end would be justified only if the person were killed from some other, ulterior motive and the claim of euthanasia was only pretense. However, that is not so in the present context.

Nor is there a radical difference between the sorts of situations men-tioned: that only in euthanasia does the person himself die whereas in all other cases he remains. The procedure is more radical in the one instance because it involves the person himself. But this is not to use the person. It is to use a radical procedure which eventuates in the radical consequence: the person's death. Alleviating the individual's misery is still the aim or end. Therefore, the ultimate end, insofar as that notion makes any sense at all, is the person himself.

In fact, it could be argued that when properly construed, euthanasia actually requires that the individual be considered as an end in himself. The objective of euthanasia, after all, is to alleviate agony or suffering. It is the result of deliberations centering around the question of which kind of treatment will produce the best positive state of affairs *for that individual person.* In other words, it is precisely because the individual is assumed to be an end in himself that a continued state of agony, indignity, and debilitation is judged unacceptable; that euthanasia becomes not just the right course of action but a duty. According to this argument, therefore, keeping the individual alive despite his condition for the sake of family or society, would actually be using him as a means to an end.

According to another objection, assigning intrinsic worth to people is based on an unworkable ethical assumption. Not that persons *are* merely means, contrary to what the argument would have us believe, but that in certain contexts we simply must abandon the notion of an end in itself as an incommensurable value and must calculate. Everyday life is not as neat and compartmentalized as the argument would have it. Potential euthanasia situations are not always characterizable by the question, Should he live or shall we liberate him from his unbearable mode of existence? For example, when medical resources are insufficient the issue is not so much whether the quality of a person's life is unbearable or whether he will be used as a means to an end. The real issue is whether he should live at all. Should we administer what resources there are on an equal basis, thereby making virtually sure that all who then and there require them will die; or should we assign these resources on a selective basis and thereby save the lives of at least a few? In such a situation there is no avoiding a decision. According to the argument of persons as ends in themselves, resources would have to be distributed equally. Anything else would be to treat those not selected as means to the survival of the ones selected. But surely such a course of action is mistaken and morally repugnant. In such a context we *must* calculate, *must* treat the death of some as the means to the life of others. Any moral theory that denies this is simply mistaken.

Finally, although this argument is based on the intrinsic worth of human beings, it ignores the quality of their lives. The life of a person—not just a human being, but a person—is seen as sacred, its destruction as a moral affront. The nature and quality of a given individual's life are apparently considered irrelevant.

However, limiting intrinsic worth to *persons* introduces the necessity for criteria. When is a person reduced to being merely a human being? Unless the concept of personhood is purely biological, qualitative distinctions between various sorts of lives based on their social and conceptual complexity, their sophistication, and the amount and degree of their awareness become relevant. These qualitative criteria must be met in order for the lives in question to count as the lives of *persons* and therefore as sacred. But then the sacredness of a person's life—its unique moral status—is not based on mere membership in the species Homo sapiens but on his mental or spiritual qualities. Other lives are not sacred because they lack such mental qualities as self-awareness.

A religious argument in favour of euthanasia might come from precisely this angle, on the basis of a distinction between human and personal life as a function of organizational and functional complexity. The argument could be based on the distinction between person and body, and might maintain that under certain circumstances we may be faced with a living body which nevertheless is no longer a person because it no longer houses the soul. If such a premise were combined with the claim that we have moral obligations towards persons only, it would be easy to infer that no religious precept—no Judaeo-Christian precept—against the killing of persons would be violated if we were to euthanatize a body from which the soul has departed.

BODY AND SOUL

Ramsey, Thielicke, and other religiously motivated writers have argued that when an individual is in a deep and irreversible coma caused by extensive and irreparable brain damage, resuscitation or sustaining efforts may cease. Karl Barth writes, "Never abandon care of the dying except when they are irretrievably inaccessible to human care." In such cases, his reasoning seems to be, we are no longer dealing with a person in the proper sense of that term but a mere human body: a biological entity that formerly was a person but now is merely alive. Helmut Thielicke states explicitly that "one should not speak in such cases of having maintained 'life.' For what is maintained is merely certain limited biological functions. To put it more pointedly, there has been a preservation of the vitality of specific organs of an unburied corpse." He concludes, vis-à-vis the disposition of such an entity, "that what is involved here is not a theological question about the nature of man but a biological question directly related to the value of the humanum." Ramsey concurs.

If the moral basis of this reasoning is correct, then the mere biological organism legitimately may be utilized for certain purposes, e.g., as a "vital organ bank." But is the position just indicated valid?

Any attempt to answer this question presupposes that we understand clearly what is here involved. In Thielicke's discussion, the term "life" refers not merely to the body's biological life processes but to another vivifying process: whatever constitutes the life of a person. In this present discussion, however, the term "life" will be used in the purely biological sense only, and Thielicke's conception will be explicitly enunciated.

The argument under discussion, then, holds that the duty of saving or sustaining life exists only towards persons, or beings who have souls. Since human beings with severe, irreversible brain damage affecting the higher brain centres (and who are therefore in an irreversible coma) are biological human beings only and not persons because they lack souls, we do not have a duty to engage in lifesaving or sustaining acts. We may let them die or otherwise dispose of them as we see fit—even use them as "living tissue banks."

The cynic would retort that this is an attempt to get around the biblical injunction "The innocent and just thou shalt not put to death" and the command "Thou shalt not commit murder," simply by making sure that by definition the individual to be killed can no longer count as a person. Prominent theologians have argued that such an approach is logically suspect.

Others, however, have supported it. Karl Rahner, for instance, has maintained that we must distinguish between an individual as a biological organism and an individual as a person. Someone whose brain has deteriorated beyond the point of functional return and whose life will be without any "personal content" must count as a live biological organism but cannot count as a person. He lacks a soul. It is not that to be a person in a religio-moral sense and to have a properly functioning brain are synonymous. They are not. Instead, the point is that the functioning brain alone provides the biological basis of personhood, which in turn makes possible the presence of a soul. In the sorts of cases just mentioned that functional basis is destroyed. Consequently, since the body no longer functions well enough to support the divine spark—namely, the soul—the individual is no longer a person in the religious sense, appearances notwithstanding.

Historically this position has the support of the church fathers. Saint Augustine claimed that the word "human" is reserved for the unity composed of living body plus human soul, and St. Thomas Aquinas held "We must say that the intellect, which is the operative principle of understanding, is the form of the human body," and continued that "It is natural for every form to be united with its *proper matter*"—where "proper matter" means the functioning, biological human body that is capable of memory and self-awareness and other ratiocinative operations. From this it follows, as St. Thomas himself mentioned in passing, there is a fundamental difference between a human biological organism, even if it should be fully developed and functioning, and a person. The former is a purely biological entity; the latter is a besouled being, a biological entity infused with a soul by God when the biological organism is of a certain nature. From this it also follows that if the biological organism is constitutionally no longer capable of memory and self-awareness then it no longer is the "proper matter" with which the form of man, the soul, can "naturally" be united. Consequently, while we would still be faced with "this flesh and these bones," we should no longer have a person.

However, even within the theological sphere, the bases of this endorsement of euthanasia may be challenged. For example, the presence of a human soul which is one of those bases, has proved impossible to establish directly. However, the fact that we can find no guaranteed criteria to establish its presence, does not prove that the soul is absent. Consequently, no one can ever justifiably claim that a given biological entity is no longer a person because he lacks a soul: The claim that he lacks a soul can never be conclusively established.

On the other hand, if a particular sort of behaviour were considered definitive of the presence of a soul, then the absence of that behaviour would indeed conclusively establish the absence of a soul and a lack of personhood. However, the price of this certitude is far too great: It would force us to say that anyone who was not actually then and there exhibiting the required behaviour did not possess a soul and therefore was not a person. The remediably comatose and the momentarily unconscious, not exhibiting the requisite behaviour, would therefore have to be considered non-persons. Most of us would find this consequence quite unacceptable.

Of course these problems could once again be avoided by referring to the potential presence of the definitive behaviour patterns, or to potential modes of communication. But in the end, the only way in which such potential-clauses could be made to work would be if some physiological criteria were given on the basis of which the existence of such potentials could be conclusively established. However, that would ultimately reduce to the claim already noted above: that the presence of a nervous system of a particular level of complexity and of a certain functional state is a necessary as well as sufficient condition for the presence of a soul.

In the end, however, this whole enterprise is really an attempt to reconcile biblical injunctions against killing with the facts of modern medicine. In other words, it is an attempt at exegesis. But unless exegesis is legitimized in actual revelation, it is merely an attempt at rationalistic, analytical interpretation. While as such it may "fittingly be proposed for belief," it lacks the revelationary certitude of dogma itself. Even the distinction between being a human being and being a person—between being an essentially biological entity and being a human being informed or infused by a soul—is itself not a matter of revealed dogma. It is a later, philosophically motivated attempt to come to grips with what in fact is revealed dogma. Biblical revelation knows only the category of man or of human being. There is here no distinct category of person. In light of this the biblical injunction against killing must be therefore reconsidered. Can we afford to gamble on the correctness of human interpretation?

The premise that we have a duty to preserve and sustain only the life of persons is also not immune from criticism. After all, if the human being person distinction goes, then the distinction of duty based on it is also nullified. Furthermore, religiously speaking the premise is simply wrong: We do have duties towards non-personal living beings, and these duties include saving or preserving their lives whenever necessary and possible. Schweitzer's principle of the sacredness of all life entails this, but so does Genesis: We are given the earth and all that is in it in trust. Not to further it as we are able, not to keep alive what we can and to take more than what we must would constitute a dereliction of this trust. It would be to confuse trust with license. Therefore, even if such patients were mere biological entities and no longer persons the duty to keep them alive may not necessarily disappear.

Finally, a problem that rose to prominence in the fifteenth and sixteenth centuries with a ground swell of mysticism is again surfacing. It is this: Both revealed doctrine and exegetical interpretation can be accepted by the individual only insofar as he understands them. In that case, however, the ultimate authority of what is religiously correct must be the individual conscience. Thus a fundamental question arises: Does this imply that there may be an irresolvable conflict between what someone takes to be the morally correct course of action according to his conscience, and what ecclesiastical authority declares to be doctrinally correct? If so, does this not suggest that when all is said and done, religious speculation cannot claim to provide the single and unique answer to the problem of euthanasia?

PERSONS AND RIGHTS

The religiously motivated attempt to make euthanasia acceptable because we are no longer dealing with persons, therefore, seems inconclusive. This attempt, however, is ultimately based on a moral, which is to say philosophical, thesis, that may be summarized like this: Someone who is effectively decerebrated, irreversibly comatose, or in an analogous state is no longer a person. However, rights and obligations, including the right to life, attach only to persons. Therefore this individual no longer has a right to life, and we no longer have a corresponding duty to save or sustain him.

This bare-bones argument is usually not stated quite so explicitly but merely hinted at or hidden behind emotionally appealing but extraneous considerations. For example, it forms the basis of Fletcher's exhortations: "Unless we face up to the facts with moral sturdiness our hospitals and homes will be mausoleums where the inmates exist in a living death." It underlies H. K. Beecher's rhetorical question, "Can society afford to discard the tissues and organs of the hopelessly unconscious patient so greatly needed for study and experimental trial to help those who can be salvaged?" It is involved in Tooley's claim that calling someone a person is synonymous with saying that he has a "serious right to life" when this is coupled with the thesis that to be a person requires "the capacity for self-consciousness." It is the ground for Engelhardt's contention that "Only self-conscious, rational beings can be moral agents, persons in this sense," from which it follows that only persons have moral duties—and rights. It is hinted at in the phrase "human vegetables;" is central to the distinction between "a corpse maintained in irreversible coma" and a person; and is fundamental to the plea that those who are alive only by courtesy of respirator, for example, and are perceptually and otherwise cerebrally quite dysfunctional be allowed to die so that the resources thus used would become available to others who are still persons. D. Arnold stated it explicitly in his article "Neomorts": Individuals whose brains are permanently dysfunctional at the higher levels are no longer persons but mere bodies that are being kept alive, and as such have no rights. He concluded that, all other things being equal, they should be utilized for pharmacological testing and medical experimentation and teaching; alternatively, they might be killed for transplant salvage or harvested for blood. The author justified this by saying that, "while it is their functioning bodies that makes them attractive as resources for the advancement of medical knowledge, it is their status (i.e., the fact that they are no longer persons) which allows us to consider utilizing them."

Like the religiously motivated version, this stance faces two problems: In order to have practical significance it must provide an acceptable definition of "personhood," and in order to be logically valid it must show that only persons have rights, in particular the right to life.

The definition of "personhood" is troublesome because it depends on the metaphysical question of the difference between the mental and the physical. Of course the debaters could decide to ignore the difference between their respective metaphysical positions and agree that they consider self-awareness and the ability to reason and engage in mentation definitive of personhood. This would indeed avoid the metaphysical problem of the nature of personhood, but only at the cost of raising another difficulty. Whereas in some instances self-awareness and reasoning powers are obvious, they are not obvious when an individual is in a coma or otherwise incapacitated, particularly when what is at issue is whether the individual is only temporarily incapacitated and therefore still a person, or whether personhood has departed altogether. Facts like sleep and temporary paralysis aggravate the problem. How are we to tell?

Advances in neurophysiology are a help. Such a close connection exists between a particular manner of functioning of the neocortex and the processes of self-awareness and reasoning that the presence of these neocortical functions has become a criterion for the capability to exhibit thought and have self-awareness. The definition of personhood from *The Practice of Death* is thus amended: A person is an entity which currently evinces self-awareness and powers of thought and reasoning in a directly observable manner such as communication; or has the present constitutional potential for these as indicated by the appropriate brain processes. Electroencephalogrammes (EEGs) are currently the most readily available means for detecting the latter. However, since certain physiological or chemical conditions in the body may suppress or mask such brain activity the following conditions should be placed on the use of EEGs: There must be a deep coma, the EEG must be flat for twenty-four hours in the absence of hypothermia, and no central nervous system depressants must have been administered.

With this, the problem of providing an unproblematical definition of personhood would seem to be solved. However, appearances are deceiving. As Thielicke has asked vis-à-vis the criterion of rational self-awareness or consciousness and its various manifestations, "Are we not obliged . . . to introduce at once a quantitative point of view and ask about various degrees of consciousness?" More precisely he asks, "What criteria would we use for deciding which life in a mental institution we are to save and which life we are not to save? These could only be pragmatic criteria." Although a religious sentiment may be the origin of this consideration, it nevertheless has moral significance. For if we define personhood on the basis of self-awareness or the constitutive potential for it we shall be committed to accepting variations in degree of personhood. This raises a familiar and horrifying spectre: first-class persons, second-class persons, third-class persons, etc. Not, to be sure, on the basis of colour, nationality or creed but on the basis of degree of cerebration.

Assuming that this problem has been solved and a definition of personhood adopted, we still face the question of rights. Is it correct that the presence of certain types of brain processes justifies the ascription of certain rights and that the absence of those brain processes justifies their denial?

Those who answer negatively see rights as a matter not of natural disposition but of social convention; hence they place the possession of rights into a social context of responsibility, contract, and obligation. Those who answer affirmatively make rights a function of desires and on that basis are willing to ascribe them to humans and kittens as well as, presumably, sharks. Of course the lines are not drawn quite so clearly. For example, some have been willing to ascribe rights to corpses on the basis of a social contract theory, whereas others have maintained that desires themselves are not enough but must involve some sort of self-awareness and ratiocination. What is clear however is that there is no consensus on the question of whether or not only persons have rights, or for that matter the right to life. Nevertheless, even if it were somehow agreed that entities other than persons have rights it could still be argued that a person's right to life always takes precedence over the right to life of anything else, and that it was not itself outranked by any other right.

Whichever of the alternatives is finally accepted, the rules and maxims underlying it must be implemented in essentially similar ways in similar contexts, without exception. This may prove unpleasant. For example, many accident victims and terminal patients presently under intensive care in hospitals or nursing homes are in fact non-persons by the definition of neocortical activity. However, consistency requires that these be treated no differently from those individuals whose bodies are needed for transplants, whose supportive machinery is required elsewhere, or whose financial burden has become too great. If the one has the right to life, so does the other, and vice versa. Likewise, with respect to death. The need for a transplant is irrelevant to whether or not an individual is a person. Lance Tibbles is emphatic:

I reject the idea of multiple definitions of death, e.g., one definition for potential organ transplant donors and a second definition for those who are not potential donors. The idea of someone being more dead than someone else merely because he has some harvestable parts, does not make a case to the common man of the objectivity of medical science.

Also, nothing in the preceding discussion has anything to do with physiognomy. The only relevant considerations deal with self-awareness, thought, and reasoning and with the criteria for determining their presence. These considerations provide no excuse for euthanatizing a radically deformed individual at any stage of his life simply because he is radically deformed. Since the presence of or constitutive potential for the characteristics indicative of personhood would justify the ascription of personhood, the right to life would follow. In fact, not even considerations of biological species will be relevant so long as the basic criteria for the ascription of personhood are met. We may not like this direction and be reluctant to accept its import; but again, from a moral point of view that is irrelevant. As Plato knew, the moral life is not necessarily pleasant. Are we, as proponents of this argument, willing to be moral, i.e., consistent?

On the other hand, it may be argued that precisely because a given individual is still a person we should, under the circumstances of irremediable, debilitating suffering or unending indignity accede to his wish for euthanasia; or if he should be mentally incapable of requesting euthanasia for himself euthanatize him even without such a request, although of course not against it. For, as [Hugh Trowell says, there is "a basic human right—the right to die, if death is the only release from suffering." We owe the person a duty of care.]

The upshot of these deliberations is this: Any successful treatment of the moral status of euthanasia requires a definition of personhood which is immune from the criticisms that have been variously raised above and which is applicable even in the hard cases of low mentality, coma, and infants. Not only that: the definition must also provide a basis for a coherent ascription of rights.

5

RIGHTS AND DUTIES

OWNERSHIP AND RIGHT

In the early days of the so-called Women's Liberation Movement, one of the more popular arguments to show that a woman had a right to an abortion on demand focused on her ownership of her body. It was argued that since she owned her body she could dispose of it and the fetus as she pleased. A similar argument in the euthanasia debate goes something like this: We own our body, and therefore our life. Since we may dispose of what we own as we please, we may do so with our body and life as well. To be sure, this may not be a legal right in the sense that the law denies us the right to purchase or sell our bodies, but it is moral right. Therefore, if the quality of our life is so irremediably bad that nothing will ameliorate it, then we as owners have the right to end it, to request euthanasia. Since each right has a corresponding duty, other people will have the concomitant duty to acquiesce in our request. Therefore, the simple fact of ownership gives everyone the right to voluntary euthanasia.

Superficially, this line of reasoning appears valid. We are tempted to say that the fundamental thesis of dispositionary power over our property is certainly correct. Also, we do seem to have a moral proprietary right to our body and life, the legalities of the matter notwithstanding. Closer examination, however, shows that both the general claim about the dispositionary rights over what is our property as well as the particular thesis that there is such a right in the case of our life and our body is mistaken. We may not dispose of our property whenever, wherever, and however we please. Any such disposition is subject to the condition that we may not harm society or other persons. This principle presents no problem in most situations. In some contexts, however, for instance where the property in question has social significance or the act of disposition itself has social ramifications, it may limit the exercise of our rights. The enjoyment of a car would here be a good example, as would the operation of a mine. In some contexts I must not operate my car as I please, nor am I permitted to give or sell it to anyone I wish. Nor may I operate my mine as I like or shut it down if the fancy strikes me. Social interests play a determining role.

The implications of this are patent. An individual's life and body are the social manifestation of his personhood and external focus of his social significance. This, however, entails that he could not claim the right to euthanasia as an unconditional and in that sense absolute right. For insofar as he is a materially apprehensible entity, his very existence has social significance—as does an act of euthanasia. Therefore even if he did own his body and even if that entailed a dispositionary right, that right could be exercised if and only if it was not overruled by the competing right of someone else or the welfare of society in general was not adversely affected.

Of course all this assumes that the individual does indeed own himself. However, it could be argued on religious grounds that such ownership resides not with us but with God; that, as G. J. MacGillivray has it, "It is our duty to take care of God's property entrusted to our charge—our souls and bodies. They do not belong to us but to God." Even St. Thomas Aquinas maintains that "Whoever takes his own life"—or, we would add, asks for it to be taken—"sins against God, just as whoever kills another person's slave sins against the slave's master." We no longer consider slavery moral, but the reasoning holds: Just as a certain piece of goods or a certain animal is property, so we too are property—the property of God—and our destruction by euthanasia or any other means is a transgression against our owner.

Considered logically, however, this reply itself is mistaken. The claim that "our souls and bodies" are the property of God conflicts with the moral premise that by his very nature no person is a thing. If that is true, then no person can be a piece of property, whether that be of God or of anyone else.

Second, the reply involves a mistake in logic. The premise that someone is a slave or a piece of property does not entail the conclusion that to kill that person or slave is to act unjustly. That consequence follows only if we also assume that, "To kill someone else's slave is always wrong," or "To destroy someone else's property is always morally reprehensible." To assume such a premise is both question begging and contrary to fact. They shoot horses, don't they? Even against the owner's will, if the horse is irremediably injured and seriously suffering? In fact, the very existence of the Society for the Prevention of Cruelty to Animals is based on the presumption of such a right, the wishes of owners notwithstanding.

On purely philosophical (i.e., moral) grounds it could be argued that we cannot own life and body because we are identical with them. We cannot *own* what we *are*. Expressions like "I am my own person!" or "I have a right to my own body!" or even "I own my body" are merely metaphorical. This of course may prompt the reply that therefore the initial inference goes through after all. If as social agents we are our bodies, then we have the moral right to self-determination and therefore may do with our lives as we please.

To reason thus, however, would be overly hasty. It may be replied that like all rights, the right to self-determination is not unrestricted. Its exercise must not harm society and must not be outranked by the competing rights of someone else. Nor will it be possible to argue that this right is different from all others and constitutes an exception because it arises from the fact that as persons we are free agents. That a free agent is capable of a particular act does not entail that he has the moral freedom, the right, to do it. Nothing physical may hinder him, but the moral status of each act must be considered separately. The question of freedom, therefore, of the right to self-determination, then, is the question of what we are morally permitted to do in a given context, and that depends on the rights of others and of society.

Therefore, the claim that we own our own life and body, even when reasonably interpreted, fails to show that we may dispose of ourselves as we please. It may be that we do have the right to euthanasia; but if we do, then whether or not we are morally permitted to exercise it must be decided from situation to situation on the basis of the moral ramifications of each individual case.

THE RIGHT TO DEATH

The right to death is sometimes claimed as a converse of the right to life. The reasoning assumes that all of us have a right to life, observes that a right is not a duty, and concludes that we may therefore refrain from exercising the right to life, i.e., that we may therefore request euthanasia without incurring moral guilt. In the words of the Voluntary Euthanasia Society, "The right to die is logically a part of the right to live. If there is no right to end one's life, then it is not a 'right' to live but an inescapable obligation."

Unfortunately, this argument is not conclusive. The first problem is that it assumes that the right to refuse to exercise a primary right—in this case the right to life—is always effective. This is not so. It is already clear that the exercise of a certain right is always limited by competing rights and its effect on society. Therefore the right may not be effective in a given instance. Like any other right, the right to life comes with a concomitant right to refuse to exercise it. Now, just as the right to life is limited by competing and perhaps higher ranking rights, so the concomitant right to refuse to live is also conditioned. It too is subject to the strictures attendant on the exercise of any right. This does not mean that when a particular right is outranked it and its concomitants disappear. All that it means is that its exercise is interdicted under the prevailing conditions. Therefore the right to refuse to exercise the right to life may also be rendered ineffective. This does not change it from a right into a duty but merely holds the exercise of the right in abeyance.

The second problem is that the argument involves a confusion between the right to refuse to exercise the right to life and the right to choose to die, which is something else entirely. An example may make this clear: If I have the right to fish in a certain pond, then, since it is a right and not a duty I have no obligation to do so. I may stay at home or go to a movie instead. However, it does not entail that I have the right to do the opposite of fish—namely, to stock the pond. That right is different from the right not to fish; it must be acquired separately. It may not be acquired. For instance, there may be ecological reasons why I should not be allowed to stock the pond, reasons which in no way affect my right to refuse to fish.

So also the right to refuse to exercise the right to life and the right to death—to euthanasia—are logically quite distinct. The former entails that I *need* not make any effort to live. It amounts to the right simply to let matters proceed along their natural (causal) course without any attempt on my part to interfere with the causal sequence of events so as to favour my living. The second, however, is not the right to let nature take its course but the right to *ensure* that the outcome of the present course of events is fatal even if that should require that I interfere with this course of events. To be sure, the practical outcome on either alternative may be the same: I may die. But it need not be. For, the failure to exercise the right to life is perfectly compatible with, say, accepting a spontaneous remission. An exercise of the right to die, however, is not. I would have to attempt to prevent a successful remission. Therefore even though the right to life does not entail the duty to live and even though it does entail the right to refuse to exercise this right to life, it does not entail the right to death—i.e., to euthanasia. The argument which presents the right to death as a logical consequence of the right to life is therefore logically mistaken. As an aside, we might also note that the initial argument also assumes that we in fact have a right to life. While the legal or constitutional basis of this may be clear, whether or not there are limiting conditions on this remains a moot point.

Finally, it is sometimes argued that someone has a right to something only if he has a desire for it, has had such a desire, or is capable of having it given his nature and present constitution. If this contention is correct, then an individual's mere desire or present capabilities of having such a desire for euthanasia would be sufficient to establish his right to death.

But is the premise correct? The proposal has found few adherents. Awareness at some level does seem to be a necessary condition for having rights; but to found rights on desires surely goes too far. It would give the burglar a right to the goods of his neighbour, the murderer to the death of his victim, and the sexually perverted to the rape of the child. It would give the insane the right to be tortured—and impose upon us a corresponding duty—and it would give the sadist the right to our agony—as well as us the duty to submit. Of course, it could be replied that as in all other cases, so here too the right is always defeasible. However, the issue is not whether the right is absolute or defeasible but whether or not it exists at all. Nothing argued so far shows that this premise constitutes an acceptable claim. On the contrary, one might well argue that rights and desires are fundamentally distinct; that rights must involve personal relations and cannot exist in a social vacuum, whereas desires can; that rights have a reciprocal nature involving corresponding duties and arise out of a social interrelationship of mutual advantage, whereas desires have nothing interpersonal about them and, being unilateral, cannot establish corresponding duties and are not based on mutual advantage. Other differences could also be raised: For example, assuming such a basis of rights, how could rights be transferred? How could a conflict of rights be resolved? How could one person's claim to having a certain right be well-founded and another's not? What is the basis on which rights could be ranked? The shortcomings are clear. As an attempt to establish the right to euthanasia, therefore, this view fails.

DUTY

Some arguments insist that in certain circumstances we have not the right but the duty to die and that others have the duty to euthanatize even if death is not requested or goes against the wishes of the individual. For instance, if someone is completely overwhelmed by the sheer agony of a situation from which he has no means of escape, kindness demands that we relieve his mental or physical suffering by killing him. Someone trapped in a burning car, a terminal cancer patient, and someone dying of Huntington's chorea are here examples. Not to kill them would be condemming them to torture in the full knowledge of a fatal outcome. The fact of moral incompetence may also compel us to a duty of euthanasia. Children, the feeble-minded, and the comatose, for instance, are not able to make such decisions for themselves, yet in some situations these decisions must be made. We as individuals must decide for them as we honestly believe they themselves would have done had they been able to do so. And given what we know or believe about their wishes, we may well have the duty to decide in favour of euthanasia. Finally, in some situations we have the duty to euthanatize not for the individual's benefit but for the sake of others. For instance, when the life of one person might be saved only with the heart from another individual who, although irremediably brain-damaged and irrevocably comatose, nevertheless could live for quite some time. Also in triage situations we have the duty to save one life—at the cost of another. We may not like this but the moral facts of the matter leave us no other choice.

The first claim, that we must kill someone out of kindness, assumes that the duty of care takes precedence over all others. But it is possible to argue that the duty of care is outranked by the duty to preserve life because life is an absolute. Another possible objection is that killing and kindness are logically incompatible, the old adage notwithstanding. There is something logically contradictory about saying that we must kill someone because we feel kindly disposed towards him or because we want to do him good. Finally, the argument assumes that the quality of life is relevant in deciding whether or not we have the duty to kill. This may be so, and reaching a nadir of existence may indicate euthanasia. Determining when that nadir has been reached, however, requires specific criteria. The lack of a way to measure quality of life makes the principle impossible to implement. Furthermore, the qualitative premise also requires explicatory and restrictive clauses about what sorts of qualitative considerations are relevant, to what degree, etc. For, presumably not all qualities will be involved in these considerations, nor will they be involved to the same degree. Unless these clarifications are supplied the argument while alright on the purely general level fails at the practical.

A similar difficulty occurs in making decisions for the incompetent. Doing what such an individual himself would wish, even if that includes euthanasia, is the ideal. Determining those wishes, however, presents a problem. Even if a living will or some previous apparently unequivocal expression in favour of euthanasia was available, the decision makers must still weigh these indications in view of the existing situation. But how will that be possible unless the general evaluative criteria that the patient would employ if he were able, are known? The difficulty, however, lies in determining these. At what point would the patient himself find his life not worth living? What aspects of his life would be valuable to him? Which would be irrelevant? How could these be translated into quantitative terms to give us the necessary decision-making apparatus? Lacking precise criteria and measurements, how could we decide when to euthanatize? If the patient never expressed his wishes, is now comatose, what is it moral to do? May we assume that the moral preferences of the community majority—if we knew that—hold in this case as well? Particularly if euthanasia seems indicated?

Another, more serious difficulty involves the question, what moral weight should be given to the wishes of the patient in the first place. The argument assumes that the patient has a right of self-determination and allows that the right may be transferred to another person. But what guarantee is there that even under normal circumstances the wishes of the patient, as an exercise of his right to self-determination, should carry any weight at all? Until the moral right to complete self-determination is proved, we have no occasion to try to formulate precise evaluative criteria that would reflect the wishes of the patient or to attempt precise measurements of the quality of his existence, much less a duty to euthanatize—at least not on these grounds.

Furthermore, there is the issue of how the wishes of a patient who is comatose or otherwise incommunicado can ever be determined, where we have no indication whatever of the patient's inclinations. This is the sort of situation where someone without any friends or acquaintances and with no known next of kin is brought in a comatose state to a hospital. Do we have the right to assume that what we ourselves would consider to be the moral preferences of the majority of members of the community hold in this case as well? Particularly if the decision would be in favour of death? Without a fully developed theory of the interrelationship between an individual and society could we really reach a coherent and morally defensible decision?

Finally, there is the argument that we may have the duty to euthanatize not for the sake of the patient but for the sake of others. The argument cites cases of transplant need and triage, and also mentions the financial or emotional burden that families of terminal patients must bear; the scarcity of medical resources in general; and the ecological strain of supporting such patients. The basic premise of this reasoning is that one individual's life must be given up for the sake of another. But that still leaves the practical problem of establishing a calculus by which to decide whose life is to be sacrificed and whether a life is to be sacrificed (or saved) at all. Without this the whole argument remains theoretical.

But even on this theoretical level difficulties obtain. It could be argued that the very possibility of such a calculus must be rejected not merely on practical grounds but also on moral ones. For any decision in favour of killing one person in order to save the life of another would literally be to use him as a means to an end. To be sure, the refusal to do so may conflict with our inclinations, particularly if the putative euthanasia candidate is in an irreversible coma whereas the recipient of the organs could otherwise lead a perfectly normal life. But these are irrelevant to a theory which identifies human beings with persons, which considers persons as incommensurables, and which places an absolute value on human life. The only way to avoid this critique would be to show that we are no longer dealing with persons. In that case, however, there would exist no moral problem in the first place.

Finally, there are objections to the suggestion that we have an overriding duty to save life even in triage contexts or when one person must be allowed to die so that another may live. Logical tidiness demands proof of such a general duty. However, the very attempt to establish its existence must fail because of the condition that only *certain* lives must be saved. This exception clause contradicts the universality of the injunction to save life. The argument need not proceed any further.

SELF-DETERMINATION

The contention that an individual has the right of complete self-determination, even to the extent of euthanasia, underlies a series of legal or quasi-legal considerations in favour of euthanasia. The presumption of Western society, particularly the English-speaking world, is that each responsible citizen has such a fundamental right. That it is well established in common law is clear from the judge's opinion in *Natanson* v. *Kline*:

Anglo-American law starts with the premise of thorough-going self-determination. It follows that each man is considered to be master of his own body, and may, if he be of sound mind, expressly prohibit the performance of life-saving surgery, or other medical treatment. A doctor might well believe that an operation or form of treatment is desirable or necessary, but the law does not permit him to substitute his own judgment for that of the patient by any form of artifice or deception.

However, the right to self-determination and therefore to the voluntary choice of death is also said to be guaranteed by statute. It is said to be but the other side of the constitutionally secured right to life. Thus, M. T. Sullivan argues that "the constitutional right securative of life encompasses the individual's right within lawful means to choose his own path of death." Any denial of this right, it is said, would therefore involve a corresponding denial of the right to life itself. Finally, some people have maintained that sheer consistency supports this right: If Anglo-American

law is really based on the principle of informed consent, then a terminal
or seriously afflicted individual may refuse a given medical service if he
so chooses as long as he understands the nature and implications of that
refusal. As Montange puts it, "The patient's right to informed consent
makes no sense without a right to an informed refusal." He concludes
that "self-determination, the basis of informed consent, implies that
a competent patient must have the right to redefine his best interests ...
Hence the patient should be able to withdraw his consent at any time and
discontinue the treatment." If this is correct, then the patient has the right
to ask to be allowed to die even if that course of action should seem unreasonable to others. The test of competence, as Montange sees it, focuses
solely "on the patient's capacity to comprehend his situation, risks, and
alternatives." He has the right to refuse to allow medical intervention, and
we have the duty to heed his wishes. For without the right of refusal
we would have not a right at all but a duty. That, however, would be inconsistent with the principle of informed consent, and it would make a
mockery of all relevant voluntary provisions in the law.

According to the argument, then, voluntary death is guaranteed by
common law, by the Constitution, and by the law's requirement of
consistency. However, the overall argument can be attacked on logical
grounds. For instance, none of the considerations deals with non-voluntary
euthanasia. Therefore at best, all the argument can establish is that voluntary euthanasia—death on request—is a right of any competent individual.
This immediately raises the question of whether or not informed consent
can ever be present in what is perceived as a potential euthanasia context.
Grave or mortal illness or debilitating and chronic suffering are frequently
accompanied by such severe psychological deviation that the patient
may act against his natural desire for life and request death. It could
be argued that because the request is the result of the patient's profound
depression it must not in good faith be honoured.

Furthermore, it may be argued that the standard of mental competence
suggested in the argument is defective: It confuses the ability to think
logically and correctly on the basis of certain premises with the ability
to assess a given situation rationally in evaluative terms. The two are not
the same. To be morally competent in a decision-making sense requires
more than the ability to reason logically on the basis of certain premises.
Many insane people can do that quite well. It also requires the ability to
detect premises that are reasonable and rational. Potential euthanasia
situations, however, are usually so stressful for the patient that it is unlikely that he will meet this condition, his ability to reason logically notwithstanding. Consequently it is doubtful the he can provide informed
consent.

As to the argument that the right to voluntary euthanasia is legally entrenched and therefore inviolate, it is based on the general maxim that if a particular practice is entrenched in a system of law then it is acceptable or correct. Merely stating that maxim, however, shows that it is too wide in scope. What is acceptable with respect to a particular legal system may not be acceptable in general. For instance, the atrocities commited by the Nazis on the Jews, by North American whites on American Indians, or by slave owners on slaves may have accorded with the prevailing statutes; but they lack the aura of acceptability which we usually associate with a legally acceptable practice. Thus something hallowed in common law or statute may not be acceptable in this higher sense—the sense embodied in the articles of the Geneva Convention, decisions of the World Court, or some resolutions of the United Nations. Euthanasia may be a legal right in the narrow sense, but the moral status of the legislation which brands it as legal is still open to question.

Turning to the notion of informed consent the reasoning appears to be that if on the basis of an informed and competent decision-making process someone wishes to exercise his right to die then no one may stop him. The assumption is that if others could gainsay that right it would be a right no longer. A right creates a corresponding duty in others; therefore the right to death can never be blocked.

However, as was said before, few if any rights are absolute. Most must be ranked with respect to the rights of others. Which right takes precedence depends on the circumstances. Therefore in order for informed consent to determine euthanasia, the argument must claim that the right to death is the highest ranking right, an absolute right. That however would be difficult to establish without begging the question. We have already seen that the right to life can be rendered ineffective by another's competing right or rights. But if the right to life can be outranked, so can the right to death. Babies who depend on their parents and tyros on an expedition in the bush whose lives depend on their guides, are examples of people whose rights might come first. It is possible, then, that while an individual may have the right to die, he might not be allowed to exercise it.

INALIENABLE RIGHTS

The critic of euthanasia may argue that, while rights in general can be ranked, some rights cannot be outranked. Founded in our very nature as rational beings, these rights are inalienable. As Thomas Hobbes writes in *Leviathan*,

Whensoever a man transfers his right or removes it, it is either in consideration of some right reciprocally transferred to himself or for some other good he hopes for thereby. For it is a voluntary act; and of the voluntary acts of every man the object is some *good to himself.* And therefore there be some rights which no man can be understood by any words or other signs to have abandoned or transferred.

Hobbes includes among these the right to resist assault on one's life and the right to resist imprisonment and arrest. He then concludes:

And therefore if a man by words or other signs seems to despoil himself of the end for which those signs were intended [namely "the security of a man's person in his life and in the means of so preserving his life as not to be weary of it"], he is not to be understood as if he meant it or that it was his will, but that he was ignorant of how such words or actions were to be interpreted.

The argument from inalienable rights, then, goes like this: Certain rights are inalienable and hence can never be removed or given up. Since failing to exercise them must indicate mental incompetence or a misapprehension of the relevant situation, they could even be called duties. The right to life is one of these. An individual cannot responsibly want to give it up. Therefore euthanasia of any kind is morally wrong: There are no exceptions.

The question of course is whether or not there are such rights. Hobbes, Locke, and Montesquieu affirm them. So does the constitution of the state of Virginia of 12 June 1776. "All men," it states, "are *by nature* equally free . . . and have certain inherent rights, of which, when they enter into a state of society, they cannot, by any compact, deprive or divest their posterity. . . ." In agreement are contemporary court decisions dealing with the rights of Jehovah's Witnesses to refuse blood transfusions.

On the other hand, one of the more telling objections that have been raised against this focuses on the difficulty of establishing the alleged connection between the nature of a person and the supposed right. As Henry Sidgewick put it, "If . . . we consider man in his social relations . . . and endeavour to determine the 'natural' rights and obligations that attach to such relations, we find that the conception 'natural' presents a problem and not a solution." Therefore it may be impossible to establish that such rights exist. In the absence of such a proof, however, the claim to a natural right becomes merely custom or a matter of conviction, losing its special status.

It may also be maintained that all rights result from conventions or contracts. In support of this it could be claimed that the hypothesis of an individual existing in a universe by himself and having a right to life—

or any other right—is absurd. Only in a social context does it
to talk of rights at all.

Furthermore, one could also maintain that the notion of s
internally incoherent. Although a duty implies a correspoi
no right can be a duty. A duty *requires* a certain act, but a right permits
it. A duty is mandatory; there is no choice. A right may be exercised
or not. Therefore to say that something is both a right and a duty in the
very same respect is to say that, at one and the same time, the relevant
act may but need not be done and that it must be done. That is a flat
contradiction. The argument from inalienable rights, however, will be
successful if and only if the alleged inalienable right to life is also a duty.
Otherwise voluntary euthanasia would still be permitted, and in cases of
incompetence another person could make the decision. In other words,
unless this contradiction is granted, most cases of euthanasia might not
be ruled out after all. Which is but another way of saying that the argument fails.

SELF-REALIZATION

It is possible to interpret self-realization as a moral obligation and to
base an argument against euthanasia on it thus: Everyone has inherent
potentials, and only by realizing these can one become a fully developed
individual. Death, of course, ends this development. Death that comes
naturally however, is not an abdication of the duty of self-realization.
It may even be considered a release from that duty. On the other hand,
deciding to die means deliberately curtailing one's self-realization. Euthanasia, especially voluntary euthanasia, must be rejected as morally evil.

This premise of self-realization as duty occurs in Plato and the church
fathers; it underlies the contemporary thesis "from everyone according
to his ability;" the parable of the talents expresses it, and Kant expounds
it as the duty to one's self:

It is not enough that a [moral] action not conflict with humanity in our
person as an end in itself: It must also harmonize with it. Now, in
humanity there are capacities for greater perfection which belong to the
end of nature with respect to humanity in our own person; to neglect
these might perhaps be consistent with the preservation of humanity as
an end in itself, but not with the furtherance of that end.

Kant argues even more explicitly:

[Man] sees that a system of nature could indeed exist in accordance with
[the maxim of indulgence in pleasure without troubling himself with the
broadening and improving of his natural gifts] . . . But he cannot possibly

will that this should become a universal law of nature or that it should be implanted in us by natural instinct. For, as a natural being, he invariably wills that all his faculties should be developed, inasmuch as they are given to him for all sorts of possible purposes.

Given these or analogously expressed premises, the argument then concludes that to kill an individual in the name of euthanasia is to interfere with the realization of these potentials, and that the individual who requests euthanasia is likewise guilty.

Although this argument has a venerable history, its premise is open to question. For instance, as came out in the discussion of inalienable rights, some hold that a duty can exist only in a social context, that it is based on the relationships between people, and that expressions like "I owe it to myself" are only metaphorical and are nothing but expressions of psychological conviction couched in moral terms.

Another objection is that if it is impossible to perform a duty, the duty does not exist. The issue of euthanasia, however, typically arises in situations of extreme suffering, physiological or psychological debility, even of stupor or coma, where the patients are simply incapable of any self-realization. Therefore the duty of self-realization cannot hold in these cases. Consequently, in such contexts euthanasia cannot be branded as morally reprehensible.

Finally, the argument assumes that because man has the potential of self-realization he also has the duty to fulfil that potential. Even granting the potential, including moral potential, and granting that one must refrain from euthanasia to realize the potential, it still does not follow that these potentials ought to be realized. That requires a premise to bridge the logical gap between the nature of the individual and his alleged duty; a premise to bridge the gap between the *is* and the *ought*. Such a premise would have to go something like this: If a person has a certain nature, then it is his duty to develop the potential inherent in that nature. However, accepting that premise would mean accepting Kant's interpretation of our nature as "given" to us "for all sorts of purposes;" it would imply that if we do not appreciate the existence of those duties we are morally blind. Neither of these is very persuasive—unless we are already committed beforehand. The duty to self-realization, therefore, becomes an unargued claim, and the conclusion that euthanasia is immoral is revealed as a questionable inference.

THE PHYSICIAN'S DUTY

The physician's duty in connection with euthanasia is often seen as the duty not to euthanatize. The argument is that the physician, by virtue of his Hippocratic oath, has the duty to refrain from counseling, aiding, or participating in euthanasia of any sort. This, so the reasoning has it, cuts the ground out from under any euthanasia legislation, since no physician could act on the basis of it without violating this oath. Since it is his sworn duty to attempt to preserve life, he may not take it. Therefore, since no one but a physician is quite as qualified to counsel or engage in euthanasia, for all practical purposes we may as well drop the whole issue.

The reply, of course, is that even if this interpretation of the Hippocratic oath were correct, the duty to refrain from euthanasia would not be absolute. It would depend on the physician's actually having taken the oath. Some physicians never do. Therefore they would not be bound by it and could practise euthanasia.

But closer consideration of the oath itself shows that even those who have taken it are not necessarily bound to refrain from euthanasia:

I swear by Apollo Physician and Asclepius and Hygeia and Panaceia and all the gods and goddesses, making them my witnesses, that I will fulfil according to my ability and judgment this oath and this covenant . . . .

. . . .

I will apply dietetic measures for the benefit of the sick according to my ability and judgment; I will keep them from harm and injustice. I will neither give a deadly drug to anybody if asked for it, nor will I make a suggestion to this effect. . . .

. . . .

Whatever house I may visit, I will come for the benefit of the sick, remaining free from all intentional injustice, of all mischief. . . .

The interpretation of "neither give a deadly drug to anybody if asked for it" is debatable. Ludwig Edelstein argues that it "can only mean that the doctor promises not to supply the patient with poison if asked by him to do so, nor to suggest that he take it. It is the preventation of suicide, not of murder, that is here implied." Edelstein locates the reason for this injunction in the general Pythagorean position that he sees as the historical basis of the oath: a position that considered all taking of life a transgression against "the divine command to life."

We should be on fairly safe ground if we claimed that no contemporary physician who takes this oath adopts the general Pythagorean outlook on life, on the nature of medicine, or on the status of the universe and man in it. For instance, no contemporary physician repudiates the knife nor promises to "hold him who has taught me this art as equal to my parents . . . and to live my life in partnership with him, and if he is in need of money to give him a share of mine, and to regard his offspring as equal to my brother's in male lineage. . . ." Edelstein has this to say about the oath as a moral document: "I venture to suggest that he who undertakes to study [the] development [of the Oath] will find it better under-standable if he realizes that the Hippocratic Oath is a Pythagorean mani-festo and not the expression of an absolute standard of medical conduct." The original meaning of the oath therefore becomes irrelevant, since physicians who profess it today are not themselves Pythagoreans; neither do they usually have any inkling of Pythagorean ethics. Instead the important question is, what does the oath entail for those who take it and who merely understand its words at face value?

Two considerations show that it does not entail that whoever takes it must refrain from euthanasia. First, the oath enjoins physicians to refrain from administering noxious substances or employing deadly techniques. But that injunction does not impose the duty to engage in life saving techniques. A simple analogy illustrates the point: The duty not to rob a bank does not entail the duty to deposit money in it.

Second, the meaning of the passage, "Whatever houses I visit, I will come for the benefit of the sick . . ." depends on the interpretation of "for the benefit of the sick." Unless it can be shown that "for the benefit of the sick" means to preserve or save his life, this clause allows the physician to let "nature take its course" and let the patient die.

That is in fact how the oath has sometimes been interpreted in recent times: as permitting passive euthanasia should the situation warrant it but as forbidding active euthanasia in any form whatever. But even this interpretation is based on an insufficiently close reading of the oath itself.

The oath begins with the assertion; "I swear . . . that I will fulfil accord-ing to my ability and judgment this Oath and this covenant . . ." The crucial phrase is "according to my ability and judgment." It conditions all the injunctions, admonitions, and prohibitions in the oath. Even the injunction to refrain from giving "deadly drugs" is governed by this phrase "according to my ability and judgment." Therefore the oath obliges the physician to use his judgment and leaves it entirely open for him to administer "deadly drugs" if in his estimation it is for "the benefit of the patient." Consequently, if a physician claims that he cannot engage in euthanasia because of the Hippocratic oath, what he must mean is that in his judgment euthanasia would in this instance not be for the benefit of the patient. In that case, however, we are morally entitled to know the basis of his judgment and reasoning. His word alone is insufficient. Nor will it do for him to say that death is always a greater evil than life and therefore can never be of any benefit to anyone. In the face of the excruciating, continuous, and unmitigated agony suffered by some terminal cancer patients, that is not at all obvious, and it must be proven in order to be morally defensible.

MORAL COMPETENCE

The argument that no decision in favour of euthanasia can involve the moral competence of any of the alleged decision-makers is not particularly widespread and in some of its parts is certainly fallacious but it brings together many reasons and arguments. It points out that because euthanasia has certain consequences a decision for it can be made in a morally competent manner only by someone who knows what it is that he is deciding; he must be rational and fully aware of what his choice means.

However, the argument continues, the patient is generally either so deeply drugged or so emotionally stressed and anxious that any decision he makes could hardly be called rational. A so-called living will on the other hand, made when the patient was lucid and rational, may not be valid because the patient may have changed his mind. As Sumner states it, "One of the most pathetic and curious facts of human existence is the tenacity with which most people cling to life; however tragic . . . and however painful in the last stages. The patient fights for his life." Wherefore, as the editor of *The Lancet* remarked, if such previous indications were considered binding it could happen that "the patient who, while well, had declared that he should be left untreated when incurably stricken may find himself stricken but still conscious, wishing after all to live as long as medical science will permit but unable to make this known." Previous rational decision, then, cannot be morally binding either. What is needed is a morally competent decision here and now. Since none such is possible under the circumstances of coma, emotional pressure, or drugs, we must face the fact that euthanasia cannot be instituted on a moral basis.

Of course, it might be argued that in some situations the patient is lucid, not drugged, and makes an apparently rational choice in favour of death. Even this situation has dangers. The patient, being rational and aware, may well feel that he is an excessive financial burden on his family. Patients are sensitive to pressures, and they may actually feel obliged to die. That feeling, however, no more reflects his true decision than it would if he had been drugged. Expressed under duress, it is not morally acceptable. Alternately, the drugs the patient is given or the poisons in his system may result in his feeling of despair and hopelessness when really there is no overwhelming cause. In this state of depression he may appear to decide competently for euthanasia, whereas in fact it is as Crane says, "merely his uremia talking."

As to the physician, his decision can scarcely be morally more competent than the patient's. He cannot be absolutely certain as to the medical facts of the case since error is always possible, and he may not be aware of all the recent developments in this particular medical area. Furthermore, with respect to the possibility of error, it must be realized that medical prognosis amounts to educated guesswork without guarantee of certainty. Spontaneous recoveries have occurred, and new developments in medical technology have saved people at the last moment. Therefore since a negative prognosis is not certain but only probable, a decision for euthanasia may cut off the possibility of remission or help. In areas of low moral risk—e.g., plastic surgery or trading in the stock market where a mistake may result in a blighted career or a livelihood lost—these are acceptable risks because these results are reparable. Euthanasia, however, results in death, and there is no repairing that.

The wishes of the patient are another problem. The physician cannot read minds. Even a trained psychologist may find it difficult to interpret the behaviour or statements of a patient, especially in situations of stress. Physicians could hardly expect to do better. To make matters worse, the physician is usually asked to decide for the patient precisely when there is no or uncertain and ambiguous communication because the patient is comatose or regressed. The physician might interpret the communication as rational, but that would be only guesswork and projection based on his own knowledge, fears, and inclinations.

The reply might be that the physician is at least more competent than anyone else to make a decision because, imperfect as his knowlege is, it is more complete than anyone else's regarding the patient's medical facts and perhaps his privily expressed wishes.

However, the retort to this is that it is simply not true that the physician is as well informed of the wishes and disposition as anyone else, or that he can interpret the data adequately. The typical modern physician in charge of terminal patients also has more than a hundred other patients. He cannot keep the myriad relevant data on each patient in mind nor even on a useable chart. The contemporary physician is no longer the lifelong family doctor of generations past who knew his limited circle of patients socially as well as medically on the basis of prolonged personal contact. However, it is only someone with such acquaintance and familiarity who can even begin to presume to know what the patient wants; even when faced with a "living will."

Then there is this to consider. The fact that medical care, hospital resources, and the physician's own time and energy are limited sooner or later creates a triage situation: The comatose, terminal, or irreparably debilitated compete with others in not quite so critical but nevertheless serious states. Can the physician faced with such a situation in his practice, perhaps even several times over with respect to the same patient, really be considered free from biasing psychological and social pressures? Can he really evaluate each such situation on its own merits and on a strictly moral basis?

This last raises a still more fundamental question. Is a physician really competent to make such a decision in the sense of being able to reason on a strictly moral, ethical plane? It may be argued that expertise in moral reasoning is not taught in the medical lecture hall, and that just as a physician would not presume competence in religious matters merely because he thinks about God or prays, or in legal matters just because he has passing familiarity with some statutes, so he must not assume competence in the field of ethics. There are ethical codes in medicine, of course, but as physicians themselves are beginning to discover, these codes result from haphazard tradition. They are no more correct for being hallowed. Furthermore, they were developed by physicians, people whose primary concern and training was the practical art of medicine, not the domain of ethics.

This essential difference between medical and moral expertise cannot be over-emphasized. Although medical data contribute to a decision on euthanasia, the decision itself is a moral, philosophical one. Although medical and socioeconomic skills and expertise may enable one to understand the data, philosophical expertise is necessary to appreciate the philosophical, moral ramifications and to draw the correct moral conclusion. By and large physicians lack that expertise. Or, if they have it, they have it in no greater measure than other people. The fact that they are called upon to make such decisions immeasurably more frequently than other people merely reflects the absence of appropriate moral decision-making bodies in our society. Unlike excellence in sports, moral expertise and correctness in judgment depends not on the frequency of practice but on the correctness and degree of understanding involved. Nazi physicians are good examples. None of them was medically incompetent or uninformed and none lacked practice; but they acted immorally. There is thus no guarantee that after a few practice judgments and initial mistakes the physician's understanding will deepen and his judgment become correct. Indeed, the practice may devolve into a consistent habit of judging in a particular *and mistaken* way. Furthermore, even if ultimately the resultant judgment is morally correct it will have become so at the cost of several people's lives: Is that morally defensible?

Several considerations may be raised in opposition to this reasoning. For instance, the contemporary physician is frequently overworked and some of his concerns about one patient may conflict with those about another, and in a triage situation the psychological, medical, and socioeconomic conditions may divert him from the moral facts of the case. Still, these problems do not make him morally incompetent. Conflicting influences abound in all walks of life, but these do not determine nor rob either understanding or freedom of the will. Therefore, moral decision-making competence may still exist. Likewise, it is true that the modern physician does not know his patient personally as well as did the family doctor, but this lack of personal attachments might actually leave his judgment less clouded, free to work only with the facts of the case. His feelings for the patient may not be very deep and his sympathetic interpretation of the patient's wishes may not be as sure, but that does not mean that his moral judgment will be any less certain. For there are no data to be had beyond those in principle available to the modern physician. The family doctor's special knowledge reduces in the end to empathy. When faced with a comatose or otherwise handicapped individual who in effect is incommunicado, there simply is no way he can actually know whether a comatose patient would prefer to live or die. The trauma of the death situation may have changed the patient's previous outlook. Therefore, neither the old-style family doctor nor the family itself can decide more competently than the contemporary clinical physician, their long-time acquaintance notwithstanding. To think otherwise is to imbue them with omniscience.

As to the physician's moral competence, it should be realized that acquiring such competence is part of his practical training. In a medical and social context geared to such decision-making he develops the necessary expertise. Furthermore, there is this overriding fact: *Someone* must make the decision. Who is better qualified to understand the relevant medical data than the physician? Certainly not the patient himself or his immediate family. Since his moral judgment is no worse than that of the others and since only he or the board on which he sits really understands the situation, only his or its decision will be appropriately well informed and thus morally competent.

The patient's decision in favour of euthanasia was also called morally incompetent due to the pressures and influences of his situation. However, the fact that the patient is under extreme psychological pressure in and by itself does not make him incompetent. People make decisions under such circumstances all the time, and their decisions are not any less acceptable. The claim that any decision in favour of death must *eo ipso* be the product of a morally incompetent mind is also questionable. The right to life which the contrary position maintains cannot exist without the corresponding right of refusal; and if the one decision is competent so is the other. If the exercise of the right to refusal were evidence of incompetence, then there would be no right to refuse. In that case the right to life would become a duty, and that remains unproven. It is more reasonable to admit that a decision for euthanasia does not by itself imply incompetence. As to the patient who is comatose or otherwise non compos mentis, here his fellow citizens must make the relevant decision in his best interest. The patient's right to decide on euthanasia becomes their duty to decide for him. Therefore so far from being *ultra vires* when making such a decision for a patient, those who do are merely exercising their duty. There does remain the problem of who specifically should make the decision. This much must be granted the argument: It is not clear that it is the physician's role to do so, present practice notwithstanding. Nor is it certain that the family has any better claim. After all, the family cannot have a proprietary interest in the patient, and the largely conventional ties of familial connection are morally insufficient by themselves to create such an obligation. But however that issue may ultimately be resolved, the fact remains: A decision must be made for the individual. The fact of non-identity with the patient himself does not render all other decision-makers morally incompetent. Even the lack of expertise in the moral arena cannot obviate this fact. For not to make a decision here is also to make a decision—by default. That too is fraught with moral danger.

6

TOWARDS A THEORY
OF EUTHANASIA

Socrates believed that the unexamined life is not worth living. Neither, one might add, is the unexamined death necessarily moral. However, most of the arguments about euthanasia examined here have turned out to be unacceptable. Some are logically incoherent, depending on emotional associations to make their point; others are based on questionable premises and therefore, although logically valid, not sound; still others overlook possible alternatives. Exposing these shortcomings makes it possible to work towards correct conclusions about euthanasia. For, to know what is wrong is not enough; we must also know what is right in order to do the right thing.

Is there a right solution to the problem of euthanasia? At least the following points have become clear: Euthanasia is permissible in certain contexts and obligatory in others. It is permissible where the patient is not yet a person or is a person no longer. It is permissible where the patient as a competent person requests it. It is obligatory where the incompetent patient cannot make that decision but any ordinary competent person would make it or where the individual's right to life is superseded by that of others, as in triage.

These general conclusions require fleshing out by moral principles, but any principles used must be logically consistent and universally applicable to human beings. An analysis of personhood and rights is also required, but this analysis must be coherent and acceptable, and the solution must work in actual cases involving triage and the feeble-minded. What follows is a position on euthanasia that fulfils these requirements generally but which in its details needs refining. It is, therefore, an interim proposal.

While persons have absolute value, they do not therefore have any rights such as the right to euthanasia. To see why this is so let us look at what "absolute value" means.

VALUE AND OBLIGATION

Traditionally we must distinguish between "relative value" and "absolute value." Something with relative value has value only according to someone's opinion of it. Absolute or intrinsic value, however, is independent of anyone's attitude. It exists by itself. For example, imagine a universe consisting solely of an object and nothing else. If that object still has value, then that value is absolute or intrinsic. As G. E. Moore argued, to see what has intrinsic value, "it is necessary to consider what things are such that, if they existed *by themselves*, in absolute isolation, we should yet judge their existence to be good." Some philosophers reject this distinction between absolute and relative value because they find the notion of absolute value itself unacceptable. We may toy with the possibility of intrinsic values, so they maintain, but this is only an intellectual exercise. Alexander Sesonske's claim that "all values are values for some living being" fairly sums up their stance.

The objection to this critique of intrinsic values has been that it confuses what people do with what they ought to do. What is actually done is no indicator of what ought to be done, as Socrates pointed out; and what is actually valued is no indication of what ought to be valued. To say that there are no absolute values because nothing is in fact valued by all people is illogical; and to argue that everything that is said to have value is in fact valued by someone is to confuse the cause with the effect.

To this argument in turn two replies are possible: First, the charge of confusion is question-begging because it assumes precisely what is at stake —namely, the distinction between the two kinds of value. Second, it may be argued that accepting absolute value means accepting also a universal system of values. However, either factual evidence must reveal this system, or we must postulate someone who sets up universal and ultimate values. Not only does this look very much like a theologically based ethics—which itself needs defense—it also fails to show that there is an absolute realm of values. If it shows anything, it shows that there is a universally valid system of valuing.

Furthermore, while it is true that a statement of obligation may be based on a statement of value, the two are not synonymous. For instance, the statement that a universe without the suffering of children is better than one that has suffering children in it may be true no matter who utters it. It is not, however, tantamount to a statement of obligation. While we would probably condemn as immoral anyone who, indulging in culinary delicacies, heartlessly witnesses the suffering of the starving children of Singapore, his denial that he had any obligation to help them would still be consistent with his assertion that the world would be better if such suffering did not take place. Why would we judge him immoral? The reply must be that most of us assume that there is a universally binding moral imperative to help those whom we are able to help. However, while that imperative may be in agreement with our moral judgment, the fact that we make such a judgment does not mean that there is such an imperative.

A similar argument applies to the distinction between facts of value and of obligation. For example, assume that persons have absolute value. If the hypothesis is correct then a universe with persons would be better than one without; but no one is therefore obliged to supply them. A deity could exist and yet not have a moral obligation to create such a world. He would have that obligation only if there is an absolute duty to make possible the greatest amount of value. And even that principle would require careful examination as to the means allowable for bringing about such a state of affairs. So, for instance, it is perfectly conceivable that when one state of affairs may involve more value than another, the means necessary for bringing about the first are morally reprehensible and the other not. Thus, although there may be a duty to bring about this "better" state of affairs, competing obligations may override it. Furthermore, the important point still remains: In and by itself no fact of value will give rise to an imperative conclusion.

The same point holds if we assume that all values are relative to individuals, reflective of their valuational stances. For, to say that something has value in that sense is really to express an attitude of preference, desire, or wish. It is not to make a moral statement. It is simply to describe how someone feels toward something.

Nor does the fact that he feels towards it in a certain way entail an obligation. Consider the example of an anarchist who values anarchical society. He thinks that he has an obligation to bring about this sort of society, but this is not because he thinks that he *values* it more than any other but because he is convinced that it *is* better, and because he thinks on independent grounds that he has an obligation to bring about the better state of affairs. Similarly, many of us value a different political system for certain countries in the Far East or Latin America without at the same time accepting that this constitutes an obligation to bring about such a system. In both the relative and the absolute sense, then, value and obligation are different and saying that something has value does not create an obligation.

Obligations, however, have the peculiar characteristic of always having rights as correlatives. If a person has an obligation to do something for a second person, then the second has a corresponding right to have it done for him by the first. It follows that if value does not entail obligation then it does not entail a right either. In the context of euthanasia, then, the fact, if it is a fact, that a person has absolute value, does not entail that therefore he has a right to euthanasia or that we have a corresponding obligation to provide it. If there is such a right, and if there is such an obligation these must have another basis.

RIGHTS

It has sometimes been argued that although there are no intrinsic values, nevertheless there are intrinsic or absolute rights: rights which belong to a human being by virtue of his nature and independently of anything else. They are sometimes called *natural rights*, and John Rawls's characterization of them may be taken as definitive. "[The ascription of natural rights depends] solely on certain natural attributes the presence of which can be ascertained by natural reason pursuing common sense methods of enquiry. The existence of these attributes and the claims based upon them is established independently from social conventions and legal norms." From natural right is said to follow natural duty or obligation, which Rawls once more expresses like this: "It is characteristic of natural duties that they apply to us without regard to our voluntary acts. Moreover, they have no necessary connection with institutions and social practices; their content is not, in general, defined by the rules of these arrangements."

Are there such things as natural rights and duties? A strong historical tradition maintains that there are. Hobbes, for example, as well as John Locke, and Montesquieu defend them, as do W. D. Ross, H. A. Prichard, and A. C. Ewing. However, the authority of these philosophers notwithstanding, the doctrine of natural rights and duties is mistaken. There are no natural rights. The reason lies in the nature of rights themselves. As even those who defend the notion of natural rights admit, a right is minimally a claim by someone on an individual to something. As Alexander Sesonske expresses it, rights are "claims validated by commitments." The underlying idea here is correct. Rights without individuals *to whom* the claims may be addressed and who are then obligated to fulfil them, are not even claims and certainly not rights. Therefore, in a universe with only one individual in it, to speak of rights would be nonsense. They do not exist in a social vacuum. Natural rights, however, would have to exist in such a vacuum and solely by virtue of the nature of the person. And this is absurd.

The theory of intrinsic rights, therefore, must be rejected. Rights are dependent on society, because they arise out of the relations in which persons stand to one another. More precisely, they are claims that may be made by certain individuals in virtue of the commitment-relations into which some other person or group of persons has entered with them. The commitments they imply need not be formalized or even explicitly enunciated. In fact, in certain instances the mere fact of continual voluntary existence in a social context may be enough. The fundamental factor, however, remains: Rights depend on a social commitment.

This analysis points to several important features of rights. Not everyone is able to have a right or to sustain an obligation. Only people capable of making decisions can enter into any such agreement. Consequently, although a community of gibbons may have definite social interrelations, not one of them is able to sustain obligations. Nor can a dog be said to have a moral duty. Similarly, not everyone is capable of possessing rights. As C. H. Whitely states, whoever has rights must also be "capable of understanding the commitment, of relying on it, and of demanding its fulfilment." Only *persons* can have rights, then, just as only persons can have duties or obligations because only persons can make and accept the relevant commitments. A right that cannot be claimed, even in principle, simply is not a right. But what greater inability to claim a right *in principle* can there be than a constitutional inability? Only in the case of persons is this not so; therefore only they have rights. Finally, someone who cannot *in principle* meet an obligation cannot be said to have that obligation. This is true because one cannot have a duty to do the impossible. Consequently only those sorts of beings who are capable of making decisions and of implementing these decisions in actions can have obligations.

How does someone acquire a duty? Sesonske summarizes three ways: Explicitly, implicitly and situationally. A formal, explicit commitment might be expressed with "I promise," "I agree to," "I commit myself to," or "I swear to." Implicit commitments, on the other hand, result from the obligation-relations into which someone has already entered, where the latter logically entail these further commitments. For example, to promise to keep someone alive entails the further implicit commitment to supply him with enough nutriments, air, and water. Last, situational duties arise when our existence in social relationships commits us to certain other acts and entitles others to expect them from us. Rawls gives the example of agreeing to play a game. We are then expected to abide by its rules and "be a good sport." H. L. A. Hart contends that obligation commitments can arise merely in virtue of membership in a social group. The most famous example, however, is provided by Socrates, who speaking in Plato's *Crito* for the Laws of Athens, characterizes his obligation to stay and suffer the death penalty as follows:

. . . any Athenian, on attaining to manhood and seeing for himself the political organization of the state and its laws, is permitted, if he is not satisfied with us, to take his property and go away wherever he likes. . . . On the other hand, if any one of you stands his ground when he sees how we administer justice and the rest of our public organization, we hold that by so doing he has in fact undertaken to do anything that we tell him.

We need not agree that we must do *anything* that is ordered, but that such situational commitments do arise cannot be denied.

Like obligations, rights too may be acquired by explicit commitment, implicit commitment, or situationally. They too arise only if a person voluntarily enters into a right-duty relationship with another. This point is crucial because from this it follows immediately that entities who are not persons can have neither rights nor duties. The reason is simply that we cannot stand towards them in the requisite sorts of relations—if indeed that hypothesis makes any sense at all; and they cannot stand in the requisite sorts of relationship towards us.

But this is not the only result that follows. Since rights are actually claims to something made by someone on someone, there are conditions on them. First, the social context influences what the very statement of the right means. Therefore all right claims tacitly presuppose that the social milieu will stay approximately the same. The statement of right must explicitly account for any exceptional circumstances.

Second, rights can be ranked as to relative effectiveness—i.e., as to which takes precedence over the other should a situation of conflict arise. All other things being equal, whichever right was established first in time takes precedence. Otherwise those rights, the exercise of which is logically presupposed by the right in question, take precedence. For instance, the right to life takes precedence over all others since it is logically presupposed by all of them: There can be no rights if there are no persons. Likewise the right to liberty is basic since the right-duty relationship presupposes that the persons are acting voluntarily.

Third, if a certain state of affairs is necessary before a right can be exercised then whoever has that right also has the right to bring about the necessary situation. This condition can complicate extensively the question of whether or not someone has a right and whether the right is effective.

Fourth, the principle underlying a right has to be universalizable without contradiction and when universalized must not make the very existence of the right itself impossible. Thus rights may not involve inherent inequities, and they may not cause society's dissolution.

Fifth, any right may be made ineffective by being outranked by another right or by being inherently impossible to fulfil under the circumstances. Again, the correlative duty must not be an impossible one.

It is also important to realize that since all rights are contractual, any right can be given up. Furthermore, because a right is a claim, it need not be exercised unless the right holder sees fit. Duties, on the other hand, must be fulfilled on demand. Somewhat differently, whereas there are no operant conditions that dictate whether or not a right must be exercised, only conditions as to when it may, there are just such conditions for duties. In fact, it is this latter sort of relationship that characterizes them as duties.

THE RIGHT TO LIFE

As we have seen, some participants in the debate argue that the right to life is inalienable, absolute, or natural; that it is without conditions and that it cannot be given up since it is rooted in the very nature of a person as a moral agent. Others argue that since there are no such natural rights then, if it is a right at all, like all rights it can be rendered ineffective or surrendered voluntarily. Some argue that there is a natural, absolute duty to save or maintain life at all cost; others maintain that if such a duty exists at all it is not absolute and other obligations can override it. Some debaters stress a duty to life, others maintain that not only is there a right but in some instances even a duty of death.

However, it follows from the position on rights sketched above that those who reject euthanasia as immoral on the basis of the assumption that there is a natural right to life (and a corresponding duty to maintain it) are fundamentally mistaken. Since there are no intrinsic natural or absolute rights, there can be no natural right to life either. The idea of a universe consisting of but one person who then claims a right to life illustrates the claim's absurdity. Only if others were to come to that universe or if there were an ideal observer to whom such a claim could be addressed would the claim make sense.

The right to life, then, like all other rights, occurs only in relation to other people. The fact of a person's existence alone is not enough to support it. What, then, constitutes its basis? One basis has already been indicated: The right to life is presupposed by the existence of all other rights. That thesis, however, is dependent on the existence of the other rights. For this reason some participants in the debate turn instead to the notion of absolute value. They argue that all beings who have intrinsic value have a right to life. As to what sorts of beings these are, here there are several variations. One such variation has it that all living beings have absolute value just because they are alive; that therefore they have a right to life, and that consequently their destruction is morally evil. This sort of position, however has traditionally been confined to the Eastern world. In the West the focus has largely been on a particular *quality* of life: namely, one involving self-awareness, "moral capacities" and the like. Thus there is a tradition which claims that all beings who have self-awareness or moral capacity have absolute value solely in virtue of these properties, and that therefore they have a right to life.

Both alternatives are unacceptable for two reasons. First, both base the right to life not on the person's relationship to others but on the person's nature. Whether that nature is merely being alive or also having self-awareness is irrelevant. To base the right to life on a person's make-up or nature however, is to return to the concept of natural rights, and that is logically unacceptable. While it may be true that only living things have a right to life, or only living things with self-awareness and moral capability, it is not true that they have that right *because* of these properties.

Second, both approaches ground the right to life in a person's absolute value. However, as we saw, having such value does not imply having the right to life or for that matter, any rights at all.

Other attempts have been made to ground the ascription of the right to life. For example, the desire to live or merely the potential for that desire has been used in that way. However, this sort of approach also fails, for according to it, the mere fact of desire itself, no matter whether it is evinced by a baby, an adult, or any other living thing, entails a *prima facie* right to what is thus desired. The redefinition of "right" implied here would have to be argued, and even if only a conscious desire would ground the right to life, it is not clear why rational awareness when added to desire should make such a difference. Furthermore, both alternatives would have to show how the potential desire for something can establish an actual right to it here and now. Also, like the preceding hypothesis, this one ignores the social context and basis of rights.

Other theories have been proposed: An individual may acquire the right to life by the services he renders to the rest of the people. An individual has a right to life because he has other rights that presuppose it. An individual has a right to life because someone who has the right in the first place or can grant it gives it to him.

These three suggestions at least recognize the fundamentally social nature of rights. In the end, however, all of them fail. The first would not allow us to ascribe rights to all individuals to whom we would want to ascribe them. For instance, more specifically, it would make it impossible for us to ascribe the right to life to a thalidomide baby or to anyone else who through no fault of his own was a ward of society from birth. Therefore, while it may correctly describe rights such as those involved in the ownership of goods and property, it does not hold for the right to life.

The second, on the other hand, is unquestionably correct as far as it goes. If the exercise of a right someone has presupposes the existence of a particular situation, then having that right gives him the right to bring about that situation. Therefore if someone has the right to freedom from torture or to freedom of speech then he also has the right to life. After all, the exercise and indeed the very existence of these presupposes his being alive. However, although this argument establishes a relationship between rights, it does not show how the initial rights themselves arise. Therefore it is insufficient as an analysis of the right to life as such.

That leaves the third possibility: that the right to life is given away by someone who has it in the first place or is granted by someone who is empowered to do so. Both alternatives provide the necessary social context. However, while in a closed environment with limited resources people might agree to add a new member only if someone else drops out, giving away his right to life, this is not how things are at present. Someone does not lose or give up his right to life merely because society acquires a new member, nor is society able to gain a new member only if someone gives up his right to life. A reranking of rights may be involved when a new member is added now but, as an analysis of how the right to life functions at the present time, this argument fails.

In retrospect, the second alternative reflects the present state of affairs more closely. Society, through the parents, grants the right to life to an individual in letting him develop to the stage of moral capability or personhood. The right to life therefore, is conferred by all those individuals who as members of society are instrumental in bringing about its existence as part of the social complex. In that sense, then, the acquisition of the right to life is situational, and continuing along the lines indicated above, this granting of the right to life carries certain commitments to the growing person. For instance, the rights to sustenance and education. Furthermore, these rights will outrank the corresponding rights of parents and other adult members of the society. However, like all rights, this right to life is also conditional in the sense that as soon as the child becomes morally competent and independent the rank of his rights is reduced to equality with that of the rights of the other adult members of the society.

From this it should be clear that someone's right to life may outrank another's as well as be outranked in turn, depending on circumstances. Furthermore, it may be given up voluntarily as may any right. Thus someone may not wish to exercise his right to life; and in most instances that decision requires no justification. Lifeboat situations are exceptions. In these the passengers' right to life outranks that of the crew.

However, since someone competent to operate the lifeboat is necessary for the passengers' survival—that is to say, since the exercise of the passengers' right to life presupposes the existence of someone competent to operate the lifeboat—at least some crew members must survive. Therefore although the crew's right to life is outranked by that of the passengers, some crew members must remain alive *even though the individuals themselves might choose otherwise*. As Judge Henry Baldwin put it in the case of *U.S.* v. *Holmes*, "The sailor is bound . . . to undergo whatever hazard is necessary to preserve the boat and the passengers. . . . The passenger cannot be bound to sacrifice his existence to preserve the sailor's. The captain, indeed, and a sufficient number of seamen to navigate the [life-] boat must be preserved; for *except these abide in the ship, all will perish*." Judge Baldwin continues: "But if there be more seamen than are necessary to manage the boat, the supernumerary sailors have no right, for their safety, to sacrifice the passengers"; and he goes on to comment about the ranking of rights: "The sailors and passengers, in fact, cannot be regarded as in equal positions. The sailor (to use the language of a distinguished writer) owes more benevolence to another than to himself. He is bound to set a greater value on the life of others than on his own." Judge Baldwin then goes on to consider some practical effects: "And while we admit that sailor and sailor may lawfully struggle with each other for the plank which can save but one, we think that, if the passenger is on the plank, even 'the law of necessity' justifies not the sailor who takes it from him."

Even the law, then, accepts the moral principle of the ranking of rights. Applied to the right to life in biomedical contexts, the same situation holds. In some cases the primary right to life with the concomitant right not to live is rendered ineffective, and life becomes a duty. In such situations voluntary euthanasia—if otherwise it was a right—is a right no longer.

To summarize: Like any other right, the right to life can belong only to a person because only persons can have rights at all. This right itself results not from some nature or property like the person's self-awareness or the presence of a wish or desire but is acquired through commitment. This requires the existence of other persons, for only persons can stand in the requisite sorts of commitment relations. Moreover, no one can have both a right and a duty towards the same individual in the same respect at the same time. Furthermore, rights are ranked and thus limited by the interplay of commitments relevant in each case.

But what of situations involving a non-member of a given society who requires medical aid in order to save his life? According to the preceding analysis it would seem that such an individual, not being a participant in the society's complex of commitment relations, has no rights at all and therefore no right to life. Consequently it would seem that the others could kill him with moral impunity or at least let him die. No moral judgment would be applicable. Presumably any medical and experimental atrocity could also be condoned as long as it occurred outside of the society's complex of commitment relations.

Objectionable as it may seem on the surface, the basic contention on which this is based is indeed correct. This strikes us as unacceptably severe. However, the severity may be mitigated by the following rather simple consideration: To admit that there is no such right (or duty) is not to admit that therefore the converse of this obtains. Furthermore, one could argue with Rawls that in the era of global society that is upon us there is no such situation as the one here envisioned. No society is isolated from any other; neither is any individual. Therefore commitment relations of some sort obtain among all persons and hence the right to life insofar as it is presupposed by all other rights holds for each person.

However, although perhaps appropriate for the world as we find it this rejoinder is clearly insufficient. The thesis itself goes against our intuition; it is objectionable because it would still allow such actions in principle, and that is the claim that must be rejected.

Two replies are possible. The first takes the form of a diagnosis. It consists in pointing out that the feeling of moral outrage is the result of a conception of the nature of rights and obligations that locates the possession of a right in general and of the right to life in particular in the mere nature and existence of the individual: The individual has intrinsic value and therefore the right to life. However, rights do not follow from value. Therefore this objection fails. Likewise with the claim that the individual has a natural right to life. Since this has also been shown to be mistaken, the feeling of outrage has emotional significance only.

The second reply focuses directly on these emotional misgivings and suggests that in fact they are out of place. It points out that in such cases we may not do what we please. On the contrary, drawing on the nature of rights as discussed previously, it concentrates on the fact that above all else, persons are rational agents. Rationality, however, implies consistency; and therefore, the universalizability of the maxims underlying the acts. This in turn entails that to depart deliberately and in full knowledge from such a mode of action constitutes a voluntary departure from or contradiction of this defining characteristic of personhood. Now, as was shown above, rights belong only to a person. Not, however, simply in virtue of his personhood, although that is one of the necessary conditions, but insofar as a person he occupies a certain place in the web of relations that constitute the particular social structure of which he is a member.

In a sense, so far as society is concerned, the individual person is identified in terms of this position. It follows that if a necessary precondition for occupying that particular relational position is no longer met, then the individual in question necessarily can no longer occupy it; whence in turn it follows that the rights and obligations definitive of that relational position no longer belong to him either. However, the deliberate repudiation of a necessary precondition for membership in such a relational complex constitutes the deliberate removal from the framework of relations itself. For instance, the deliberate repudiation of citizenship constitutes a repudiation of all those rights and obligations that are concomitants of citizenship, just as the deliberate refusal to fulfil the necessary condition of playing according to the rules of chess and in a rational manner calculated to win is tantamount to a resignation from the game itself. Likewise, the deliberate departure from or contradiction of the defining characteristic of personhood amounts to a deliberate repudiation of one's status as a person so far as the complex of social relations is concerned. Therefore, whoever acts in such a manner thereby voluntarily removes himself from the web of relations which he as a person occupies. In other words, the individual who deliberately acts in a manner contrary to a defining characteristic of personhood, which is a necessary precondition of rights and obligations, abandons his relational place and thereby gives up those rights and obligations which otherwise belong to him in virtue of occupying that particular place.

This does not mean that the individual voluntarily ceases to be a person altogether. Although in a way that is possible—when someone deliberately kills himself or destroys his intellectual capabilities—obviously what is meant here is different. The place of an individual as a bearer of rights and obligations depends not merely on his ability to act rationally, i.e., as a person, but on his perceived status as actually doing so, when appropriate. Therefore it is his voluntary giving up of the perceived person status that is here at issue.

In this way, then, and for this reason, anyone who acts in the way indicated voluntarily places himself outside of the system of duties and rights. Constitutionally he may still be a person, but functionally he no longer occupies that status and therefore will no longer count as a repository of rights and obligations.

The implications of this are obvious. To be sure, a person who is not a member of society has no moral right to any help. At the same time, however, anyone who treats him in a way he would not treat members of the society who do have such rights is treating him in a manner in which he himself would not like to be treated as a person and which, when universalized, would cause the disappearance of society itself. Consequently he would be treating such an individual according to a maxim that could not be universalized consistently. This however, would be to engage in a deliberately irrational act, and therefore would be to contradict a defining characteristic of his role as a person. He would therefore be voluntarily abandoning his status as a member of the system of rights and obligations. Although a response of retribution would in a strictly moral sense be inappropriate, treatment of him as though he were no longer a part of the system of rights and obligations would be correct. The consequence of this could be unpleasant, since the action would effectively place him in the same position as the individual who is outside the domain of rights and obligations.

Thus although there is no moral duty to treat all persons as though they had rights and especially as though they had the right to life, there is what might be called a counsel of prudence to that effect. It is simply prudent and in the interest of preserving one's own moral status as someone who has rights to act in this way. Of course, as Rawls suggests, very few if any situations will involve a mere reliance on this counsel of prudence. To all intents and purposes society is global. Socioeconomic interactions make it so. The principle, however, must stand.

The preceding is just a sketch. However it shows that the preceding analysis of the right to life does not lead to absurd consequences. The theory's outcome does not conflict seriously with what intuitively seems morally correct. Nothing in it is logically unacceptable, and cross-cultural ethical situations support it.

However, a central part of this analysis is the concept of a person. So far that notion has received no explicit discussion.

PERSONS

The concept of a person which is central to moral contexts is that of a being that has at least the following characteristics: self-awareness, rationality, symbolic awareness of reality, and the capability of language, awareness of itself as a free causal agent, and volition. Let me consider these in turn. Without self-awareness an individual cannot be a moral agent. The concept of moral agency—of someone who of his free will acts in certain ways—depends on it. Awareness without self-awareness may be possible but it would not play any role in a moral context. The ability to think, or rationality, is necessary because without it there cannot be any understanding of a given situation or of the actions possible in a given state of affairs. It provides the ability to choose among possible actions and to appreciate their results. Without thought an individual would respond to a stimulus in a Pavlovian way, and any assignment of moral responsibility for an act would be out of the question. Symbolic awareness of reality means the ability to distinguish between the self and the rest of the world. Without it the individual would quite literally be his own world. Symbolic awareness, by its very nature makes language possible; anyone who has it also has the capability for language, although he may not necessarily be using it. Strictly speaking, the idea of morality also requires that the individual *be* a free agent, not just that he think of himself as one. Without this the individual would be strictly determined in all his actions and any ascription of responsibility in a properly moral sense would be impossible. An awareness of this free causal agency is required because otherwise the action will be based on an inherent assumption of determinism, and although in fact free, nevertheless the individual would lose that awareness which is necessary for the ascription of responsibility. Finally, will is necessary because without it the individual could not convert his decisions into action.

No other characteristics are necessary. A person may have neither likes nor dislikes but still proceed towards given ends. He need not even experience love, hate, fear, or joy. We might consider such a person less human than others, but he would still have personhood. Otherwise, someone who had attained a state of pure mental detachment would no longer be a person—which is absurd. At the same time, these characteristics are sufficient because they make it possible to ascribe moral responsibility to whoever or whatever has them. It is important to note that nothing in the characteristics necessitates a particular physiological constitution. In fact, they do not even imply the existence of a material constitution at all. Any being who possesses them is a person in a moral sense.

How to discern these attributes is usually no problem. The individual's behaviour and way of communicating usually settle the issue. Not that we formally evaluate them. It is more that the awareness of these is so interwoven into the structure of our perceptions that apprehension of someone as a person (or non-person) is usually automatic. The problems arise in borderline cases. Not only in those in which it is not quite clear whether the charactistics are met fully but also in those where it is not immediately or directly obvious that they are present at all. Sometimes sleep, anesthesia, or temporary coma—even a deep meditative trance—mask them even though they are present. All other things being equal, individuals in whom they are thus present though hidden nevertheless count as persons in a moral sense, and retain their rights and duties.

The problem, then, is how to include them in the definition of persons. There must be something common to them which unquestionably indicates personhood but which cannot automatically be identified. That element might also be a guide in the remaining borderline cases.

What the people who do not exhibit the criteria but must nevertheless be counted as persons have in common is a constitutive potential for evincing these characteristics. That is to say, we can distinguish between various degrees of potentiality. For instance, the hydrogen atoms in an interstellar gas cloud are potentially other elemental atoms such as gold, bismuth, or zirconium, and may be transformed into these by a fusion reaction. More distantly, they are potentially a tree; for all the material of a tree comes by the same process from primeval hydrogen in the interior of a sun. The tree, of course, is a potential chair, house, or firewood. Of course, realizing one set of possibilities for the hydrogen atoms from among the myriad open to them rules out a whole set of others. In this way the hydrogen atoms' becoming carbon atoms rules out their ever becoming, say, common table salt or a porcelain cup. Therefore pure potential describes the almost unlimited possibilities open to the primitive mass of interstellar hydrogen. Conditioned potential is more limited. The seed of a tree has such limited potential. The plan for its development is already inherent in its structure. It can become nothing but a tree. It is in this conditioned sense that a fertilized ovum is a potential human being. Constitutive potential is even more circumscribed. For example a computer which is not at the moment operating has such constitutive potential, or alternately a computer which is operative but without the input necessary to activate its various programmes. The computer has possibilities, limited by circuitry and the nature of its programmes, but these remain only potential until the computer is activated and the appropriate input supplied. However, this sort of potential does not require a change within the computer's make-up. It involves only activating what is already there.

We can characterize the fundamental similarity between awake, sleeping and comatose persons by saying that the former have the same constitutive potential for rational brain processes as the latter. The only difference is that while in normal and awake persons this potential is actualized, in comatose or sleeping persons it so far remains potential. Furthermore, it is possible to identify the capability for these brain functions. The brain's electrochemical activity, recorded on electroencephalogrammes (EEGs), has a characteristic structure. That of a normal human being accepted as a person is different from that of any other living thing. According to neurophysiological investigations this sort of activity is not shown by just any kind of brain; it requires a properly functioning neocortical brain structure which is like that belonging to a normal person. Otherwise normal but sleeping or temporarily unconscious persons have such brains. It is just that their full functioning is potential only—held in abeyance, as it were. Waking up or recovering actualizes the potential, and the other defining characteristics of a person become normally observable.

Thus, someone is a person in the morally acceptable sense only if either he is currently self-aware, rational, symbolically aware of reality and capable of language, aware of his freedom to act, and possesses will— where these characteristics are directly observable in a behavioural manner or are indicated by the presence of the appropriate characteristic neurological activity; or he has a brain which is structurally and functionally similar to that of a normal human being, particularly with respect to the neocortex or its relevant analogue, and therefore has the constitutive potential for these characteristics. This definition includes all those individuals who are normally considered persons in the moral sense, possessing rights and duties. The temporarily unconscious or comatose will count as persons just as long as their nervous systems show the constitutive potential that persons have. So with sleepers, infants, or anyone else. The definition excludes anyone who does not and by his present neurological constitution cannot have the defining characteristics.

It is now clear what rights and duties are, what defines a person and what it means to say that only persons have rights. It is also clear that whereas only persons have rights, not all persons do; and that a person may voluntarily give up a right, like the right to life; or that this right may not always be effective. These findings lay the groundwork for dealing with euthanasia.

VOLUNTARY EUTHANASIA

Does an individual have the right to decide that he does not want to live any longer? That he either wants to be killed outright or allowed to die? And is the claim to such a right effective? In a word, does he have a right to death?

Strictly speaking, the answer is no: There is no such right within the framework of fundamental rights and obligations. However, this is not to say that *in effect* there is no right to death, for each person as a member of society has the right to life and with it the concomitant right to refuse to exercise it. All other members of society, therefore, have the corresponding duty to make it possible for him to refuse to live; the duty to allow him to die. Furthermore, each person has the right to freedom from torture; and that gives each the further right to bring about whatever is necessary to free himself from torture, even if that should be death. Finally, each person has the right to self-determination; and while the universalizability criterion that governs all rights prevents us from concluding that therefore this right allows all acts of self-destruction or all requests for such, still, when the individual himself rationally decides there is no other alternative, self-destruction is morally acceptable.

In this derivative sense, then, each person within society has the right to death. But as we saw, no right is absolute. Therefore just as any right may be outranked by another's competing rights, so too the right to death may be outranked and rendered ineffective. For example, children, wholly dependent on a parent for their survival have a right to life that supersedes the parent's right to death. The children's right to life presupposes the availability of parental care, and as long as the parent can ensure the children's survival, even if he is seriously ill or in agony, he may not morally exercise his right to death. Similarly, the life of a group of survivors may depend on the knowledge and experience of their guide, who is agonizingly debilitated with, say, a broken spine. Their right to life however, outranks his right to death. Therefore so long as his existence makes their existence possible, his right to death is rendered ineffective. However, since it is his living as a source of information and not his living as such that makes their survival possible, his right to death again becomes effective when he can no longer help them.

Situations in which the right to death is outranked are, however, exceedingly rare. Usually only someone else's right to life outranks it, and even here the right to life does not automatically take precedence. Whether someone has the duty to remain alive very much depends on the interrelationship among the rights of the individuals and the question of whose right is here effective.

Some of the arguments in the preceding chapters adduced the fact of unconsciousness or coma as a reason for not euthanatizing even though the individual was the author of a living will and all other indications were that if he could make the decision there and then, he would opt for that death. The reason given was that not only was there the possibility of diagnostic error, but also and indeed mainly that the individual might have changed his mind and be unable to communicate this. However, it is now clear that the patient, insofar as he is still a person, still has a right to death. His incapacity does not nullify that right; it can only be outranked; and presumably that is not here the case. Of course, given his present situation he cannot exercise that right, nor is it completely certain that if he were conscious he would wish to do so. However, two factors may impose a duty of euthanasia: Part of the system of moral interrelationships is that if an individual is incapable of disposing of his rights, other suitable members of society have the duty to administer these for him to the best of their ability. Therefore in such situations we have the duty to consider whether under the circumstances euthanasia would constitute the correct exercise of the person's right, the necessary information is supplied by the living will or other indications to the same effect. To be sure, the individual may have changed his mind since he wrote the will. However, it is highly unlikely that any such change will be as cool, deliberate, and well-reflected as the initial decision itself which, under ordinary circumstances and as proposed by the various voluntary euthanasia societies, would be considered a true expression of the person's opinion only after thorough consultation and a period of reflection. Furthermore, if the person had changed his mind it would have been his duty to inform those apprised of his previous opinion and to invalidate his living will. Not doing so would constitute a dereliction of his duty towards his fellow person. Just as it is his right to decide for or against a living will (euthanasia) and the duty of his fellow persons to see that this decision is carried out, so it is his duty not to deceive them about his decision and to do all he can to make it correctly known. As to the possibility that the patient had changed his mind at the last moment and although willing to inform his fellow person did not have the time to do so, the conclusion would still be correct. There is always the possibility that the patient has changed his mind, even at the last moment of consciousness, and if that possibility were grounds for refusing to engage in euthanasia, no living will could ever be honoured. This, however, would mean that there would be no right to death in the sense previously spelled out: no right to refuse to exercise the right to life and no right to self-determination, for a right which cannot ever be exercised is not a right. This argument is therefore logically unacceptable. Which of course, is not to say that the patient never changes his mind. It is to say that those who assume that the person has not changed his mind cannot be held morally guilty.

Finally, because no one can have a duty to do what is impossible no one can have a duty to make absolutely certain, beyond the slightest possibility of error, that the patient has not in fact changed his mind. It is impossible to have such certitude in any human decision-making context. For instance there is always the possibility of misunderstanding. What is required is that the decision-makers apprise themselves of as much information as is relevant and reasonably possible to obtain under the circumstances, including what is known about the patient's attitude, and that they be guided by what they think are the best interests of the patient. That is all that it is possible to do. In proceeding thus they will have discharged their moral duty. In fact, not doing so would be a dereliction of that duty since there is the patient's living will that expresses his desire to exercise his right to death.

Of course, in some situations an individual's expressed desire for euthanasia is not morally binding on others. For instance if the patient is an incompetent adult or a child, then although he may clearly and unequivocally have expressed a desire for euthanasia this desire cannot be considered determining: The individual is morally incompetent. Instead, the decision must be made as it is for comatose or unconscious individuals.

These last are not instances of voluntary euthanasia. The fundamental feature—informed consent—is missing. Instead a decision for euthanasia here would be an instance of non-voluntary euthanasia in the strict moral sense.

INVOLUNTARY EUTHANASIA

Is non-voluntary euthanasia, imposed without a competent person's request or even against it, morally acceptable? The answer is yes, but we must distinguish between two sorts of cases: involuntary euthanasia where the patient is incapable of making the decision himself and has never previously given any indication of his wishes; and non-voluntary euthanasia, where irrespective of the patient's wishes the decision must be for death.

Involuntary euthanasia divides further into two kinds: those where the individual is still a person but because of coma or drug-induced stupor cannot decide for himself and those where the patient is no longer a person. Because living wills are not now common legal instruments, those who lie drugged in terminal cancer wards, subsist feebly and or mindlessly agonized in intensive care units, or hooked up to a respirator and other supportive machinery and hovering on the edge of death—in a word—have not made a living will. Therefore whoever must decide about euthanasia for them cannot merely implement a decision already made. In other words, he cannot claim to be merely an executor. The decision will be unequivocally his. He must decide what to the best of his knowledge an ordinary person of the patient's social background would choose. He must then decide whether anyone else has a competing and higher-ranking right. Since that is highly unlikely, a decision for euthanasia would be as effective as if the patient himself had made it. Consequently the duty to euthanatize would follow. It requires no separate discussion to see that from a purely moral point of view the cases mentioned a few paragraphs ago—morally incompetent adults and children who opt for (or against) euthanasia—fall into this category. They must be treated as though there were and could be no indication of their wishes. In their case, therefore, the decision-making burden falls to the appropriate responsible agency.

The second sort of involuntary euthanasia probably would not be called euthanasia at all except for custom. Personhood is essential for euthanasia, and in these cases the patient is no longer a person.

That is to say, the conclusion of the preceding discussion of personhood was that the behavioural criteria for being a person are functionally dependent on the presence and operation of a particular kind of nervous system or brain. For this reason the mere absence of the associated behavioural characteristics themselves was said to be insufficient to establish the absence of personhood. A separate and independent proof was needed to show that the functional neurophysiological basis was missing. This, so it was concluded, could be done in either of two ways: by proving extensive and irreparable structural as well as functional damage to the neo-cortex, or by showing that the relevant electrochemical activity of the brain (as indicated by an EEG) was no longer within the complexity limits characteristic of a person. Effectively decerebrated accident victims, heroin overdose cases, and those with brain deterioration due to oxygen deprivation, all fall into this category in these and similar cases. The physiological basis of personhood is no longer present. Consequently we are no longer dealing with persons at all but with (artifically kept alive) biological organisms: with mere biological members of the species Homo sapiens. Since only persons have rights, and these biological organisms do not have any, they do not have the right to life either. Consequently, the duty to keep them alive which is owed to persons is not owed to them. Of course this does not mean that there is never a duty to keep such individuals alive. After all, duties owed to other members of society might require that they be sustained. But this duty is not the converse of their patient's right to life. Therefore in most instances that fact, as well as the almost universal scarcity of high-grade medical resources and personnel and the presence of *persons* who do have a right to medical care make it a duty to euthanatize.

NON-VOLUNTARY EUTHANASIA

The distinguishing feature of non-voluntary euthanasia is that it involves the duty to euthanatize even though the individual is a person and may not wish to die. This happens in triage and when a patient's right to life is outranked by someone else's rights.

There is no question that when medical resources are limited physicians select which patients to help and which to let die. Instead the question is whether such a practice is morally defensible. It is sometimes objected that to select at all is to deny the right to life of one person and in fact to use him as a means. The competing individuals ought to receive equal treatment even if, as unfortunately may frequently happen, it should result in the death of both. This is one of the inescapable tragedies of human existence.

However, this argument betrays a misunderstanding of both triage and the nature of rights. In triage equal treatment in the sense of sharing is physically impossible; and distributing resources equally results in the death of both. Common sense calls this absurd. The issue is really this: If both people have equal competing rights to life, is it possible to act at all without arbitrarily and unfairly deciding that one's right outranks another's and thereby violating the second individual's right? Furthermore, since any action requires such an unfair ranking is it possible to act at all without incurring moral guilt? Must we not here obey the general maxim that where moral action is impossible we have a duty not to act at all?

The answer is no. It is possible to act without becoming morally guilty because the alleged impossibility of action lies not in any physical impossibility but in the moral guilt which supposedly would accompany any selection. Allegedly, the guilt would result because to select one person over another would be to treat their rights as not equally effective, thereby willfully contradicting the true state of affairs. However, if their rights could be ranked without contradicting the presumption of equality, action would be possible without moral guilt, and common sense would be satisfied. There is a way to achieve such a ranking: Simply by assigning each right an equal degree of probability then and drawing lots. In that way the equality of rights would not be denied and the duty of action which common sense insists could be fulfilled without anyone incurring moral guilt.

That still leaves the question whether any selection procedure, no matter what its basis, does not ultimately treat all those who are not selected as means. The answer is that such a conclusion involves a basic confusion over the nature of rights. All rights are conventional and depend on the social relationships of the people involved. Furthermore, their effectiveness depends on the fulfilment of certain circumstances or conditions. It is because of this fact that rights can be ranked and have different degrees of effectiveness. Therefore, when one person's right renders another's ineffective the second person is not being used as a means for the satisfaction of the right of the first. Instead the circumstances necessary for the first person's right are met, whereas those of the other's are not. Therefore the selection procedure in and by itself does not reduce anyone to a means. Neither does the decision procedure of the previous paragraph. Any such reduction would have to occur in the resulting act. The selection process itself has nothing demeaning about it.

Finally, there is the question whether there is a duty to develop an artifical ranking procedure when the rights involved are equal. Is drawing lots to decide who shall live in such cases a violation of the equal rights of those who are not selected?

The logic of rights implies that this is not the case. For, competing rights entail conflicting duties. This, in turn, implies that there is indeed a duty to act in such cases. The only question is which one of the competing rights is effective, which one of these conflicting duties must be fulfilled.

How, then, to rank the conflicting rights to life? Five considerations provide an answer. First, since a duty that is impossible to fulfil is not a duty and neither is the corresponding right effective, if one of the patients cannot be saved at all with the available medical facilities then he loses his right to life. Second, morally speaking the loss of personhood is tantamount to death. Therefore, if the one patient could live but would lose his personhood because of the resulting cerebral deterioration whereas this would not be the case with the other, then the medical intervention in the first case must be construed as foreseeably unsuccessful. Consequently the first patient's right to life is thereby rendered ineffective. The second person's otherwise equal right will outrank the first's and selection must go that way. Third, the quality of life facing the patients is a consideration. If in the one case the prognosis upon successful intervention is for an agonized, grossly deformed, disfigured or otherwise unbearable existence which to the best knowledge and understanding of the appropriate decision makers neither they nor any other normal individual would want to live, then the available resources should be given to the other person. There is merely a duty of care for this patient. Fourth, the right to life of a person necessary to the survival of a group of persons ranks higher than that of any one of the group. His survival is the circumstance necessary for them to exercise their right to life, whereas this is not true for any one of the remainder. Thus a crew member would be chosen over a passenger in a lifeboat, a guide over one expedition member, and so on. Fifth, if saving one person drains the family's or society's resources more than would saving the other, causing a correspondingly larger drop in the quality of their lives, then that individual should not be selected.

UTILITY

None of these criteria are in any way startling or constitute a radical departure from common sense. Their only advantage is that being parts of a larger conceptual whole, they provide us with reasons and understanding of why such practice is correct. And insofar as they do that, they fulfil the Socratic requirement of a moral and meaningful action. However, there is one consideration that I have not mentioned as a criterion but which occurs frequently in discussion of euthanasia in general and in triage in particular: Utility.

It is sometimes argued that whoever is of greatest usefulness to society should be the one saved. This principle of utility is said to provide a workable criterion for euthanasia.

There are two reasons for rejecting it: The first is the internal difficulty of how to define and evaluate utility or value in a given case; the second is the much larger problem of the nature of utilitarianism itself.

All utilitarianism assumes that individuals have a calculable value, that this value depends on their usefulness to society, and that the greater this value the greater the person's rights. At least, this is presumed to be so when it is a question of life and death: If one individual contributes or is likely to contribute more to the welfare of society than another, then the existence of the first has greater value than that of the second, and consequently the former has a greater right to life than the latter.

The approach promises to set the whole selection process on a calculable basis. However, all other things being equal, it is precisely this calculable basis that is unacceptable. For it supposes that rights can be derived from utility or value, and not only assumes that the former are logically dependent on the latter but also that in some lawlike and hence predictable way they are commensurate. However, neither of these assumptions is correct. Rights are logically quite distinct from values and vice versa. For instance, rights can be transferred, exercised, or held in abeyance, but values cannot. Values can be mathematically added, but rights cannot, and whereas a particular person may be of great value to society, from this it does not follow that he has any greater rights. In short, rights and values are on entirely different logical plains. Therefore the claim that the precedence relations among rights are a function of the corresponding precedence relations among values is also mistaken. Whence it follows that the question of which person's right to life takes precedence or is effective in a given context, therefore, is not a function of which individual has greater utility: i.e., is of greater value to society. It is a function of the relations among the rights themselves. It may happen that a person's value to society coincides in degree with his right to life, but that will be a matter of happenstance only, not of the logic of the case.

The preceding also suggests a solution to the problem of whether it is morally acceptable to euthanatize a person for the sake of society. To put in terms of the preceding, does society's collective right outrank the individual's right? The answer is that rights cannot be summed in any arithmetic sense, nor is the relationship between the effectiveness of one right and a conflicting group of rights a matter of summation. An example should make this clear. The fact that five people each are owed a debt of five dollars and that a single person is also owed such a debt does not mean that if the five were to ask for their due collectively as a group their debt would have greater claim than that of the single person. In these and similar cases the issue must be decided on the basis of which claim or right ranks higher—a situation which will require that the constitutive rights of the members of the group claim be opposed *seriatim* to that of the individual. It is only when at least one of the former outranks the latter that the latter is rendered ineffective. In other words, it is not because the collective representation qua sum outranks the individual, but because the individual right is outranked by the individual right of one of the members of the group. The notion of a collective right as the sum of individual rights, therefore, is a fiction. Possibly it results from confusing rights with values; possibly from confusing the legal fact of group action and the collective damages sought with the strength of the collective action based on individual claims evaluated separately and in turn.

Applied to the problem of euthanasia, this means that the utilitarian solution to the opposition between the right to life of an individual and the welfare of the community as a whole, based on the notion of collective rights, is mistaken. Therefore the individual may be euthanatized for the sake of the community if and only if the rights of the individual members of the community considered each by each outrank the right of this individual in at least one instance. Otherwise his right to life remains effective even should the world be at stake. It is *not* the case that he must die, morally speaking. It may be a good thing morally if he voluntarily chose to do so, but that is another issue—a question of whether it is morally good not to exercise a given right. It is not however a matter of obligation.

In the preceding pages I have sketched a theory of euthanasia which differs from others in that it is based on presupposition of rights rather than on utilitarianism; it denies the notion of natural rights and yet manages to accord the right to life or its equivalent to all persons; it is not tied to Kant's notion of a categorical imperative but at the same time is able to use his universalizability criterion; and so on. Furthermore, it also includes a distinction between being a member of the human species and being a person. But philosophical coherence is not enough. Any moral theory must eventually meet the test of practice. This theory works in the cases of voluntary euthanasia and the comatose or otherwise incompetent as well as in triage situations. It was designed to do so. Whether it has general validity however, is still open to question. Infanticide can serve as a test problem for the developed theory as a whole. The theory has no built-in bias in that respect so far because infanticide has not been discussed at all.

INFANTICIDE

"Infanticide" here means the deliberate killing of the newborn. It accords not with the legal treatment of any minor as an "infant" but with *Black's Law Dictionary*, which calls infanticide "the murder or killing of an infant soon after its birth." Is infanticide a species of murder? To put it in a nutshell, that all depends. Is the infant a person? Not all infants are. Although all infants are members of the species Homo sapiens, not all of them meet the defining criteria for personhood. Is the infant's right to life effective? Others' rights may outrank it. Does the duty of care require euthanasia or medical help? Qualitative considerations are here relevant. And so on. In short, if the theory that I have sketched is correct there is no hard and fast answer. It all depends on the circumstances that obtain and on how they are related to the general principles that have been outlined.

I shall expand on this in a moment. Before doing so, however, I must remove a possible source of confusion rooted in the preceding questions. Together with their replies they entail that at least some infants are persons. However, so it may be argued, although some infants do have a rudimentary self-awareness and while most of them do have the ability to internalize language none has rationality or is aware of its freedom to act or of itself as distinct from the rest of the world. Therefore it may be argued that none has a right to life and all may be killed. This, however, is so radically at variance with ordinary opinion that any theory leading to such a conclusion must be rejected.

This initial objection however, fails on two grounds. First purely logically speaking, the fact—if it is a fact—that such a conclusion would be contrary to common opinion and belief does not show that it (as well as the theory on which it is based) must be rejected. What is at stake is a point of ethics not of commonly accepted belief. Nevertheless, credibility hinges on common acceptance. Fortunately, therefore, the analysis entails no such conclusion. For—and this is the second reply— this sort of criticism completely ignores the point that personhood can depend either on the actual possession of these criteria or on the constitutive potential for them. This consideration, useful in decisions regarding the comatose, paralyzed, and otherwise incapacitated, also supplies an answer in this context: Most infants do count as persons because, although they do not actually show an awareness of themselves as distinct from others, and so on, they do have the necessary potential.

What, then, is the solution to the problem of infanticide, and how is it justified? To begin with, infants who are not persons do not have rights, including the right to life. If no one else's rights require keeping them alive, those encephalic or severely brain-damaged neonates whose neocortical function is so severely and irreparably inhibited that they do not have a constitutive potential for rationality, will, self-awareness, symbolic awareness of reality, capability for language, and awareness of their freedom to act—in short, those infants who lack the defining characteristics of personhood—should be euthanatized. I say "should" not because the absence of the right to life creates a duty to kill. Rather, the scarcity of medical resources creates a dilemma: Help the person or help the non-person. It is the person who has the right to medical attention, not the non-person. Therefore the duty to offer help to someone who is an infant-person is in effect the duty to euthanatize the infant who is not a person in order to conserve medical resources. They are needed to fulfil the right to life of those who are persons. Of course, if there were sufficient medical resources to go around the need for exclusive choice would disappear, and the conclusion might well be different.

The problem of infants who are persons is more complex. It involves the distinction between involuntary euthanasia and non-voluntary euthanasia. Involuntary euthanasia is the duty of care owed to unconscious persons or those otherwise unable to make decisions about their own welfare but whose rights are unquestioned. A. R. Jonsen sums up the sort of situation that falls under this rubric as follows: "Life preserving intervention must be understood as doing harm to an infant who cannot survive infancy or who will be in intolerable pain, or cannot participate even minimally in human experience." Like persons who are morally incompetent, such infants need to have their rights administered for them. In these situations life-saving and sustaining treatment would constitute what Engelhardt calls an "injury of continued existence." It would be the same as a violation of a competent adult's right to death. In other words the qualititative parameters of the lives of these infants may well be such as to make death the only release from an unbearable existence. The decision in favour of euthanasia would therefore be no more and no less than what we should expect a competent person to decide were he in a position to make such a decision. Again, I hasten to add that this need not be invariably the case, but if a reasonable person would choose it given the diagnosis and prognosis, then it will be as though the infant himself had chosen it, and it will be right as well as obligatory to act on it.

The complications of competing rights and scarce medical resources, however, usually transform situations of involuntary euthanasia into situations of non-voluntary euthanasia where the determining factors are not the rights of the infant person alone but also involve the rights of others. These may take precedence under the circumstances, outranking the infant's right to life or otherwise rendering it ineffective. For instance, other infants may be less debilitated and more likely to survive but nevertheless require immediate medical attention. Also, the impossibility of saving the infant would render his right to life ineffective even if medical resources are not scarce. This must not be misunderstood. It does not translate into a duty to kill. Nor for that matter, does it cover all rights normally associated with an infant. For instance, there is still the duty of care which is normally owed to infants, and neither the parent's right to a peaceful night's sleep nor the nurse's desire for an easy shift would outrank it. The competing rights must here be weighed: the desirability of surgery for other patients, the need to distribute resources. There is, however, no obligation to prolong the infant's life. Of course there will always be some uncertainty in making these decisions. But as we saw, that is inherent in any decision-making in the moral sphere. Therefore although there is a large area in which the moral position is clear, there is also a grey area where making a decision means taking a chance.

By way of concluding, I should like to consider two recent proposals about the disposition of "defective" infants. According to Gustafson, an infant severely afflicted with Down's syndrome or otherwise mentally seriously defective should be euthanatized "for the good of the infant, for the sake of avoiding difficulties for the family and for the good of society." Jonsen, on the other hand suggests adopting ". . . a social policy that (withholds) legal personhood from certain carefully defined categories of high risk infants until a clear diagnosis and prognosis can be made concerning them." Both suggestions are of dubious acceptability. As to the first, if nothing else is wrong with the infant, then everything depends on its degree of mental deficiency. If it disqualifies the infant from personhood, then infanticide will be permissible and may even be obligatory. On the other hand, if it does not disqualify it from personhood then there is a prima facie duty to keep the infant alive. By its personhood acquired in a social context—the fetus was allowed to become a person instead of being aborted—the infant has acquired a right to life. That right will be effective unless a competing right supersedes it or unless it is impossible to keep the infant alive. Inconvenience or even hardship, however, are not sufficient reasons for euthanasia in such cases. However, this does suggest that the nature of social support services must be restructured so as to relieve the family from bearing the brunt of this ultimately social responsibility. It also suggests mandatory genetic counseling and amniocentesis to avoid such situations. As to those cases in which mental deficiency is not detectable before birth, the answers remain: euthanasia (infanticide) if the infant is not a person or if he is but his right to life is rendered ineffective; state support and care if he is a person and his care presents problems.

Withholding personhood, on the other hand, is a wholly unacceptable solution because it construes personhood as a convention that can be given or withheld depending on the pragmatics of the situation. This may be possible legally, but not morally. The personhood of an infant is not a matter of the legal conventions we choose to employ—or refrain from employing—but a question of factual criteria: namely those criteria indicated above. If the infant meets the criteria of personhood, he has a right to life. That right is ineffective only if someone else has a higher right or the right is impossible to fulfil. Without these, infanticide is murder.

All of this has implications far beyond the immediate sphere of euthanasia. The nature of rights and personhood affects the domain of social responsibility as it is currently conceived, and extends into the whole spectrum of problems centering in the concept of the rights of individual persons. This, however, should not be surprising since the problem of euthanasia really focuses on two fundamental issues: What is a person? and, What are the rights and duties of a person? Any attempt to solve the problem of euthanasia—Is it right? Is it wrong? When? Why?—that does not begin by addressing itself to these general issues will be an ad hoc measure, designed to treat only a particular problem without paying heed to the general moral framework within which an answer must be given. Without an integration into such a general framework there will be no guarantee that what is considered an acceptable or merely practical course of action in this sphere is in fact morally correct.

NOTES

Numbers at left indicate text pages

1. THE ACT OF EUTHANASIA

11 Veatch, *Death, Dying and the Biological,* p. 99.
11 Connery, p. 18.
12 Sade, p. 864.
12 Ramsey, pp. 151-52.
12 Kirchheimer, p. 618-19.
13 *Ibid.,* p. 623
13 Veatch, p. 18.
15 Aristotle, Book 3:5 (113b #30-114a #3).
16 Callahan, p. 423.
16 Anglican, p. 17.
18 Pope Pius XII, pp. 397-98.
19 Connery, p. 18.

19 Preston Williams, p. 41.
19 Mannes, p. 31.
21 Pastoral letter, p. 336.
21 Ramsey, p. 132.
21 Pope Pius XII, pp. 393-98.
21 Kelly, "The Duty," pp. 204, 219.
23 Karnofsky, pp. 9-11.
24 Regier, p. 10.
24 Kelly, *Medico-Moral,* p. 129.
24 Cooke, p. 907.
24 Voluntary Euthanasia Society of Great Britain in Trowell, *The Unfinished Debate,* p. 168.

2. EUTHANASIA AND THE INDIVIDUAL

30 Francis Bacon, *Advancement of Learning,* p. 163.
31 S. Gorovitz et al., eds., *Moral Problems,* p. 243.
31 R. H. Williams, p. 88.
31 Trowell, *The Unfinished Debate,* p. 130.
32 Inge, p. 373.
32 Pope Pius XII, p. 393.
32 St. Augustine, *On the Nature of the Good,* p. 407.
32 St. Augustine, *The City of God,* 11:22.
32 St. Thomas Aquinas, *Summa Theologica* 1:22:2.

33 G. H. Joyce, *The Principles of Natural Theology,* ch. 17.
33 Thielicke, "The Doctor", p. 165.
34 J. V. Sullivan, *The Morality,* p. 73.
34 Anglican, p. 21.
34 Ortega y Gasset, *The Revolt of the Masses,* p. 98.
34 Harris, p. 128.
34 Anglican, p. 22.
39 Lohman, p. 97. (Author's translation.)
39 Sumner, p. 145.
40 Engelhardt, "Euthanasia", p. 170.

chapter 2 (continued)

42 Veatch, *Death, Dying and the Biological,* p. 182. Author's emphasis.
43 Regier, p. 10.
43 Ramsey, p. 161.
45 Maguire, p. 89.

47 Joseph Fletcher, as reported in Press Release of the Office of the Governor of the State of Oregon, February 28, 1972.
48 Gorovitz et al., *Moral Problems,* p. 234.

3. EUTHANASIA AND SOCIETY

52 Bodenheimer, p. 209.
53 Roux, p. 343.
55 Kirk, p. 315.
56 Jean Dabin, "General Theory of Law", p. 234.
57 Gould and Craigmyle, p. 88.
57 Kamisar, p. 1031.
58 Hume, *An Enquiry,* Sect. VIII, Part II, p. 96.
59 Maguire, p. 184.
59 Bodenheimer, p. 207.
59 *Declaration of Human Rights* quoted in Bodenheimer, p. 207, n. 5.
59 Rawls, pp. 3-4.
60 Board of Science and Education of the British Medical Association in Maguire, p. 155.
60 Author's emphasis.
62 Veatch, "Death and Dying", p. 6.

63 Montange, p. 1649.
63 *Ibid.,* p. 1634.
63 Justice Schroeder quoted in Montange, p. 1634.
66 Slater, p. 354.
66 Fletcher, p. 130.
67 John Stuart Mill, *Utilitarianism,* (L.A.P., 1957,) pp. 11, 13.
70 Weinstein, p. 29.
72 *Ibid.,* p. 29.
73 Schweitzer, p. 247. Author's translation.
73 *Ibid.,* pp. 345-49
73 R. H. Williams, p. 88. Author's emphasis.
74 Maguire, *Death,* p. 6.
75 Kamisar, pp. 1044-45.
78 Fletcher, "Devices", p. 130.
78 R. H. Williams, p. 88.
79 Fletcher, "Devices", p. 130.

4. PERSONHOOD

82 Schweitzer, p. 339-40. Author's translation.
82 Kant, p. 429.
83 *Immanuel Kant: Groundwork of the Metaphysics of Morals* (H.J. Paton translation) p. 105. Author's emphasis.
86 Ramsey, p. 161.
86 Thielicke, "The Doctor," p. 176.
87 St. Thomas Aquinas, *Summa Theologica,* 1.76.1c.
87 St. Thomas Aquinas, *Summa Contra,* 2.83.10.

89 Fletcher, "The Patient's," p. 64.
89 Beecher, "Scarce Resources," p. 2.
90 Tooley, p. 52.
90 Engelhardt, "On the Bounds", p. 51.
90 Arnold, p. 213.
91 Kluge, *The Practice,* p. 88.
91 Thielicke, "Doctor as", pp. 167, 193.
92 Tibbles, p. 732.
93 Trowell, *The Unfinished Debate,* p. 30.

5. RIGHTS AND DUTIES

95 G. J. MacGillivray, "Suicide and Euthanasia," p. 10.
95 St. Thomas Aquinas, *Summa Theologica,* 3.64.5c.

96 Voluntary Euthanasia Society of Great Britain, p. 170.
101 Natanson v. Kline in Montange, p. 1634.

chapter 5 (continued)

101 M. T. Sullivan, p. 216.
102 Montange, p. 1648-53.
103 Thomas Hobbes, *Leviathan,* 1:14.
104 *Ibid.,* p. 112.
104 Henry Sidgwick, *The Methods of
      Ethics,* (London, 1907), p. 82.
105 Kant, p. 48.
105 *Ibid.,* p. 41.

107 Edelstein, pp. 3-8.
107 *Ibid.,* p. 15.
108 *Ibid.,* p. 64.
109 Sumner, p. 143.
109 *Lancet,* 10 January 1976,
      pp. 76-77.
109 Crane, p. 170.

6. TOWARDS A THEORY OF EUTHANASIA

115 Moore, 112.
117 Rawls, pp. 505, n 30.
117 *Ibid.,* pp. 114-15.
117 Sesonske, p. 79
118 C. H. Whitely, "On Duties," in
      J. Feinberg, ed. *Moral
      Concepts* (Oxford, 1970),
      p. 56.
118 Sesonske, pp. 80-82.
119 Plato, *Crito,* 51d.

123 U. S. v. Holmes, 1842, 23 Fed.
      Cas. 360. Circuit Court,
      Eastern District Pennsylvania.
      Author's emphasis.
139 Jonsen, p. 760.
139 Engelhardt, "Euthanasia and
      Children", p. 170.
140 Gustafson, pp. 544-5.
140 Jonsen, p. 758.

BIBLIOGRAPHY

J. Agate, "Ethical Questions in Geriatric Care: Rights and Obligations of Elderly Patients," *Nursing Mirror and Midwives Journal* 133 (November 12, 1971).

Shana Alexander, "They Decide Who Lives, Who Dies", *Life* (November 9, 1962).

W. F. Anderson, "Elderly at the End of Life", *Nursing Times* 69 (Feb. 8, 1973).

Anglican Church Information Office, 1975: *On Dying Well.*

Aristotle, *Nicomachean Ethics.*

D. Arnold, "Neomorts", *University of Toronto Medical Journal,* 54:2 (January, 1977).

David Bakan, *Slaughter of the Innocents: A Study of the Battered Child Phenomena* (San Francisco, 1971).

B. Barber, "Experimentation with Humans", *The Public Interest* 6 (Winter, 1967).

T. P. Barbetta *et al.,* "Euthanasia: A Survey of Medical Opinions", *University of Toronto Medical Journal,* 44:4 (February, 1976).

Karl Barth, *Church Dogmatics* (Edinburgh, 1961).

W. H. Baugham *et al.,* "Euthanasia: Criminal, Tort, Constitutional and Legislative Considerations", *Notre Dame Lawyer* 48 (1973).

H. Beecher, *Research and the Individual* (Boston, 1970).

–––. "Scarce Resources and Medical Advancement", *Daedalus* (Spring, 1969).

S. I. Benn, "Infanticide and Respect for Persons", in Joel Feinberg, ed., *The Problem of Abortion* (Belmont, 1973).

L. J. Binkley, *Contemporary Ethical Theory* (New York, 1961).

R. Blake, "On Natural Rights", *Ethics* 36 (1925).

Edgar Bodenheimer, *Jurisprudence: The Philosophy and the Method of the Law* (Cambridge, 1967).

Dietrich Bonhoeffer, *Ethik* (Munich, 1956).

F. H. Bradley, *Ethical Studies* (Oxford, 1962).

R. B. Brandt, "The Concepts of Obligation and Duty", *Mind* 73 (1963).

E. M. Burns, *Health Services for Tomorrow* (New York, 1973).

J. Gonzalez Bustamente, *Euthanasia y Cultura* (Mexico, 1952).

Daniel Callahan, *Abortion: Law, Choice and Morality* (New York, 1970).

A. M. Capron and L. R. Kass, "A Statutory Definition of the Standards of Determining Human Death: An Appraisal and a Proposal", *University of Pennsylvania Law Review* 121 (November 1972).

H.-N. Castañeda and B. Nakhnikian, eds., *Morality and the Language of Conduct* (Detroit, 1965).

M. A. Cawley, "Euthanasia: Should it be a Choice?" *American Journal of Nursing* (May, 1977).

J. R. Connery, "The Moral Dilemma of the Quinlan Case", *Hospital Progress* 56:12 (December 1975).

R. E. Cooke, "Whose Suffering?" *Journal of Pediatrics* 80 (1972).

W. A. Cramond, "Psychotherapy of the Dying Patient", *British Medical Journal* (August 15, 1970).

Diana Crane, *The Sanctity of Social Life* (New York, 1975).

W. J. Curran, "Legal and Medical Death—Kansas Takes the First Step", *New England Journal of Medicine* 284 (1971).

Fred Davis, "Uncertainty in Medical Prognosis: Clinical and Functional," *American Journal of Sociology* (July, 1960).

L. H. de Wulf, "Organ Transplants as Related to Fully Human Living and Dying", in P. Williams, ed., *Ethical Issues in Biology and Medicine* (Cambridge, 1973).

E. F. Diamond, " 'Quantity' *vs.* 'Sanctity' of Life in the Nursery," *America* 135 (1976).

Alan Donagan, "Informed Consent in Therapy and Experimentation," *Journal of Medicine and Philosophy* 2:4 (December 1977).

A. B. Downing, ed. *Euthanasia and the Right to Death* (London, 1969).

R. S. Duff and A.G.M. Campbell, "Moral and Ethical Dilemmas in the Special Care Nursery", *New England Journal of Medicine* 289 (1973).

Ludwig Edelstein, *The Hippocratic Oath: Text, Translation and Interpretation* (Baltimore, 1943).

H. T. Engelhardt, Jr., "Euthanasia and Children: The Injury of Continued Existence", *Journal of Pediatrics* 83: 170 (1973).

———, "On the Bounds of Freedom", *Connecticut Medicine* 40:1 (January, 1976).

Ethical and Religious Directives for Catholic Health Facilities, No. 28.

J. Feinberg, *The Problem of Abortion* Belmont, 1973).

J. Fletcher, *Morals and Medicine* (Boston, 1954).

———. "The Patient's Right to Die "in Downing, 1969.

Philippa Foot, "The Problem of Abortion and the Principle of Double Effect", *Oxford Review* 5, reprinted in S. Gorovitz, *et al.,* eds. *Moral Problems in Medicine* (Englewood Cliffs, 1976).

A. B. Ford, "Casualities of our Time," *Science* 203 (January, 1968).

Renée C. Fox, "Training for Uncertainty", in Merton, Reader and Kendall, etc., *The Student Physician* (Harvard University Press, 1975).

W. K. Frankena, *Ethics* (Englewood Cliffs, 1963).

J. M. Freeman, "To Treat or Not to Treat: Ethical Dilemmas of Treating the Infant with Myelomeningocele", *Clinical Neurosurgery* 20 (1973).

L. Gale, "The Right to Die", *Forum* 9 (April, 1936).

G. B. Giertz, "Ethical Problems in Medical Procedures in Sweden," in E. W. Wolstenholme and M. O'Conner, eds., *Ethics in Medical Progress: With Special Reference to Transplantation* (Boston, 1966).

T. Goodrich, "The Morality of Killing," *Philosophy* 44 (1969).

S. Gorovitz and A. MacIntyre, "Toward a Theory of Medical Fallibility", *The Journal of Medicine and Philosophy* 1:1 (March, 1976).

J. Gould and L. Craigmyle, *Your Death Warrant?* (Chapman, 1971).

Germaine Grisez, *Abortion: The Myths, the Realities and the Arguments* (New York, 1970).

Group for the Advancement of Psychology, *The Right to Die: Decisions and Decision Makers* (New York, 1974).

J. M. Gustafson, "Mongolism, Parental Desire, and the Right to Life," *Perspectives in Biology and Medicine* 16 (1973).

Hannibal Hamlin, "Life or Death by EEG," *Journal of the American Medical Association* 190:2 (Oct., 1964).

F. Harder, "The Psychopathology of Infanticide", *Acta Psychiatrica Scandinavia* 43 (1967).

Bernard Häring, *Medical Ethics* (Notre Dame, 1973).

Errol E. Harris, "Respect for Persons," in R. T. de George, ed., *Ethics and Society* (Garden City, N.Y., 1966).

C. A. Hart, *Thomistic Metaphysic* (Englewood Cliffs, 1957).

H. L. A. Hart, "The Ascription of Rights and Duties", *Proceedings of the Aristotelian Society* 49 (1948/9).

A. Hartman, "Das ethische Urteil über die Tötung missgebildeter Kinder", in *Aktuelle Probleme des Lebensschutzes durch Rechtsordnungen.*

Edwin Healy, S. J., *Medical Ethics* (Chicago, 1956).

M. D. Heifetz and C. Mangel, *The Right to Die: A Neurosurgeon Speaks of Death With Candor* (New York, 1975).

David Hume, *An Enquiry Concerning Human Understanding*
———, *Dialogues Concerning Natural Religion.*

W. I. Inge, *Christian Ethics and Moral Problems* (London, 1972).

A. R. Jonsen *et al.*, "Critical Issues in Newborn Intensive Care: A Conference Report and Policy Proposal" *Pediatrics* 55:6 (June, 1975).

Yale Kamisar, "Some Non-religious Reasons Against Proposed Mercy-Killing Legislation", *Minnesota Law Review* 42 (May, 1958).

Immanuel Kant, *Foundations of the Metaphysics of Morals* (Prussian Academy Edition).

D. A. Karnofsky, "Why Prolong the Life of a Patient With Advanced Cancer?, *C. A. Bulletin of Cancer Progress* 10 (January-February, 1960).

Gerald Kelly, *S. J., Medico-Moral Problems* (St. Louis, 1958).

———, "The Duty of Using Artificial Means of Preserving Life", *Theological Studies* 11 (June, 1950).

I. M. Kennedy, "The Kansas Statute on Death–An Appraisal" *New England Journal of Medicine* 285 (1971).

Otto Kirchheimer, "Criminal Omissions", *The Harvard Law Review* 55 (1942).

R. Kirk, "Politics of Death," *National Review* 23 (March 23, 1971).

E. J. Kleinholz, Jr., "The Right to Die," *Virginia Medical Monthly* 103 (Feb. 1976).

E-H. W. Kluge, "Infanticide as the Murder of Persons," in Kohl, *Infanticide.*

———, "Selective Allocation of Scare Medical Resources and the Principle of Double Effect", *Proceedings of the 13th Conference on Value Inquiry* (Geneseo, 1979).

———, "The Definition of Death," *University of Victoria Occasional Papers* I (Victoria, 1975).

———, *The Practice of Death* (New Haven, 1975).

———, "The Right to Life of Potential Persons," *Dalhousie Law Journal* 3 (January, 1977).

Peter Knauer, "The Hermeneutical Function of the Principle of Double Effect", *Natural Law Forum* 12 (1967).

Marvin Kohl, *Infanticide and the Value of Life* (Buffalo, 1978).

———, *The Morality of Killing* (New York, 1974).

———, "Understanding the Case for Beneficient Euthanasia," *Science, Medicine and Man* 1 (1973).

Elisabeth Kübler-Ross, *On Death and Dying* (New York, 1969).

H. Kutner, "Due Process of Euthanasia: The Living Will Proposal", *Indiana Law Journal* 44 (1969).

S. Lack and E. Lamerton, eds., *The Hour of Our Death* (Chapman, 1975).

Dorothy Lee, *Freedom and Culture* (Englewood Cliffs, 1959).

C. I. Lewis, *An Analysis of Knowledge and Valuation* (Lasalle, 1946).

Thomas Lohmann, *Euthanasie in der Diskussion* (Patmos, 1975).

P. H. Long, "On the Quantity and Quality of Life–Fruitless Longevity", *Resident Physician* 6 (April, 1960).

John Lorber, "Criteria of Selecting Patients for Treatment", *Fourth International Conference on Birth Defects* (Vienna, 1973).

———, "Selective Treatment of Myelomeningocele: To Treat or not Treat?" *Pediatrics* 53 (March, 1974).

P. H. Long, "On the Quantity and Quality of Life", *The Medical Times* 88 (May, 1960).

Charles McFadden, *Medical Ethics* (Philadelphia, 1967).

Alasdaire MacIntyre, *A Short History of Ethics* (New York, 1966).

Richard McCormick, "Ambiguity in Moral Choice" in McCormick and Ramsey (1978).

———, *"To Save or Let Die: The Dilemma of Modern Medicine"*, *Journal of the American Medical Association* 229 (1974).

———, "The Quality of Life, The Sanctity of Life", *Hastings Center Report* 8:1 (February 1978).

R. A. McCormick and Paul Ramsey, eds. *Doing Evil to Achieve Good* (Chicago, 1978).

Daniel Maguire, *Death by Choice* (Garden City, N. Y., 1974).

———, "Right and Wrong of Mercy Killing", *Literary Digest* 124:23 (October 23, 1937).

J. T. Mangan, S. J. "An Historical Analysis of the Principle of Double Effect", *Theological Studies* 10 (1949).

Marya Mannes, *Last Rights* (New York, 1974).

J. Margolis and C. Margolis, "On Being Allowed to Die", *Humanist* 36 (Jan/Feb. 1976).

A. I. Melden, *Essays in Moral Philosophy* (Seattle, 1958).

R. K. Merton, *Social Theories and Social Structure* (New York, 1957).

Charles H. Montange, "Informed Consent and the Dying Patient", *Yale Law Review* 83 (July, 1974).

G. E. Moore, *Principia Ethica* (Cambridge, 1962).

Kai Nielsen, *Ethics Without God* (New York, 1975).

T. J. O'Donnel, "The Morality of Triage", *Georgetown Medical Bulletin* 14 (August, 1960).

Pastoral letter of the Bishops of West Germany, "Das Lebensrecht des Menschen und die Euthanasie", *Herder Korrespondenz* 29 (1975).

G. W. Paulson, "Who Should Live?" *Geriatrics* 28 (March 1973).

J. Pells, "Prolonging Life" *Nursing Times* 70 (March 21, 1974).

Pope Pius XII, "Prolongation of Life" *Osservatore Romano* 4 (1957).

H. A. Prichard, *Moral Obligation* (Oxford, 1957).

Proceedings of the Fourth International Congress on Birth Defects (Vienna, 1973).

Karl Rahner, "Gedanken über das Sterben", *Arzt und Christ* 15 (1969).

Paul Ramsey, *The Patient as Person* (Yale University Press, 1970).

F. T. Rapaport and Jean Dausset, eds., *Human Transplantation* (New York, 1968).

John Rawls, *A Theory of Justice* (Cambridge, 1971).

R. B. Reeves, "When is it Time to Die? Prologue to Voluntary Euthanasia", *New England Law Review* 8 (1973).

Hilda Regier, "Judge Rules. . .", *Journal of Legal Medicine* 3:10 (November-December 1975).

Nicholas Rescher, "The Allocation of Exotic Lifesaving Therapy", *Ethics* (April, 1969).

———, "Allocation of Scarce Medical Resources" in Gorovitz *et al., Moral Problems in Medicine* (Prentice Hall, 1976).

P. F. Resnick, "Child Murder by Parents: A Psychiatric Reflexion on Filicide", *American Journal of Psychiatry* 126 (1964).

W. D. Ross, *Foundations of Ethics* (Oxford, 1939).

———, *The Right and the Good* (Oxford, 1930).

G. H. Roux, "Aspects of Medical Ethics", *South African Journal of Medicine* 49 (March 8, 1975).

W. W. Sackett, Jr., "Death With Dignity", *Southern Medical Journal* 64 (March, 1971).

R. M. Sade and A. B. Redfern, "Euthanasia", *New England Journal of Medicine* 292:16 (April 17, 1975).

Albert Schweitzer, *Kultur und Ethik* (Munich, 1960).

Alexander Sesonske, *Value and Obligation* (New York, 1964).

J. B. Sheerin, "Mercy Killing", *Catholic World* 170 (February, 1950).

Helen Silving, "Euthanasia: A Study in Comparative Criminal Law", *University of Pennsylvania Law Review* 103 (1954).

J. Sinton, "Right to Die?" *Nursing Mirror and Midwives Journal* 139 (July 26, 1974).

Eliot Slater, "Health Service or Sickness Service?" *British Medical Journal* 4 (Dec. 18, 1971).

G. K. Smith and E. D. Smith, "Selection for Treatment in spina bifida cystica", *British Medical Journal* 4 (1973).

P. Sporken, *Menschliches Sterben* (Düsseldorf, 1972).

St. Augustine, *On the Customs of the Church.*

———, *On the Greatness of the Soul.*

———, *On the Nature of the Good.*

———, *The City of God.*

St. Thomas Aquinas, *Summa contra gentiles.*

———, *Summa Theologica.*

C. L. Stevenson, *Ethics and Language* (New Haven, 1944).

E. K. Suckiel, "Death", *Journal of Medicine and Philosophy* 3:1 (March, 1978).

———, "Death and Benefit in the Permanently Unconscious Patients: A Justification of Euthanasia," *Journal of Medicine and Philosophy* 3 (March, 1978).

Norman St. John-Stevas, *The Right to Life* (Hodder and Stoughton, 1963).

J. V. Sullivan, *Catholic Teaching on the Morality of Euthanasia* (Washington, 1949).

———, *The Morality of Mercy Killing* (Newman Press, 1950).

M. T. Sullivan, "The Dying Person: His Plight and His Right" *New England Law Review* 8 (1973).

F. B. Sumner, "Biologist Reflects on Old Age and Death", *Scientific Monthly* 61 (August, 1945).

Helmut Thielicke, "The Doctor as Judge of Who Shall Live and Who Shall Die", in Kenneth Vaux, ed., *Who Shall Live? Medicine, Technology, Ethics* (Philadelphia, 1970).

———, *Theologische Ethik* (Tübingen, 1964).

Lance Tibbles, "Is He Dead? Should He be Allowed to Die? Who Decides?" *Connecticut Medicine* 39:11 (November 1975).

Michael Tooley, "A Defense of Abortion and Infanticide", in Joel Feinberg, ed., *The Problem of Abortion* (Belmont, 1973).

Richard Trammell, "The Presumption Against Taking Life", *Journal of Medicine and Philosophy* 3:1 (March, 1978).

Hugh Trowell, "Attitudes of and Towards Dying", *Canadian Medical Association Journal* 87 (September 1962).

———, *The Unfinished Debate on Euthanasia* (London, 1973).

Richard Trubo, *An Act of Mercy: Euthanasia Today* (Nash Publishing, 1973).

J. A. Vale, ed., *Medicine and the Christian Mind* (London, 1975).

Nancy Vaughn, "The Right to Die", *California Western* 10 (1974).

Robert M. Veatch, "Death and Dying: The Legislative Options" *The Hastings Center Report* 7 (October, 1977).

———, *Death, Dying and the Biological Revolution:* Our Last Quest for Responsibility (Yale University Press, 1976).

Duncan Vere, "Euthansia" in J. A. Vale, ed. *Medicine and the Christian Mind* (London, 1975).

Jorgen Voigt, "The Criteria of Death, Particularly in Relation to Transplantation Surgery", *World Medical Journal* 14 (1967).

F. Wallsend, "Licensed to Kill?" *Catholic News* 32 (1971).

Mary Warnock, *Ethics Since 1900* (Oxford, 1966).

L. Weatherhead, *The Christian Agnostic* (Hodder and Stoughton, 1965).

Leonard Weber, *Who Shall Live?* (New York, 1976).

M. C. Weinstein and W. B. Stason, "Allocating Resources for Hypertension", *Hastings Center Report* 7 (October, 1977).

Glanville Williams, *The Sanctity of Life and the Criminal Law* (New York, 1957).

Preston Williams, ed., *Ethical Issues in Biology and Medicine* (Cambridge, 1973).

R. H. Williams, *To Live and to Die: When, Why, and How?* (New York, 1974).

W. P. Williamson, "Should the Patient be Kept Alive?" *Medical Economics* 44 (January 1967).

Jerry B. Wilson, *Death by Decision* (Philadelphia, 1975).

M. F. A. Woodruff, "Ethical Problems in Organ Transplantation", *British Journal of Medicine* 1 (June, 1964).

INDEX